AIR CAMPAIGN

BATTLE OF BRITAIN 1940

The Luftwaffe's *Eagle Attack*

DOUGLAS C. DILDY | ILLUSTRATED BY GRAHAM TURNER

Osprey Publishing
c/o Bloomsbury Publishing Plc
PO Box 883, Oxford, OX1 9PL, UK
Or
c/o Bloomsbury Publishing Inc.
1385 Broadway, 5th Floor, New York, NY 10018, USA
E-mail: info@ospreypublishing.com

www.ospreypublishing.com

OSPREY is a trademark of Osprey Publishing Ltd, a division of Bloomsbury Publishing Plc.

First published in Great Britain in 2018

A CIP catalogue record for this book is available from the British Library.

ISBN: PB: 9781472820570
           ePub: 9781472820594
           ePDF: 9781472820587
           XML: 9781472826039

18 19 20 21 22   10 9 8 7 6 5 4 3 2 1

Index by Sharon Redmayne
Typeset in Adobe Garamond Pro, Futura Std, Sabon and Akzidenz-Grotesk Condensed
Cartography by bounford.com
3D BEVs by The Black Spot
Diagrams by Adam Tooby
Page layouts by PDQ Digital Media Solutions, Bungay, UK
Printed in China through World Print Ltd

Artist's Note

Readers may care to note that the original paintings from which the colour plates in this book were prepared are available for private sale. All reproduction copyright whatsoever is retained by the Publishers. All enquiries should be addressed to:

Graham Turner, PO Box 568, Aylesbury, Bucks, HP17 8EX, UK, or www.studio88.co.uk

The Publishers regret that they can enter into no correspondence upon this matter.

Imperial War Museums Collections

Many of the photos in this book come from the huge collections of IWM (Imperial War Museums) which cover all aspects of conflict involving Britain and the Commonwealth since the start of the twentieth century. These rich resources are available online to search, browse and buy at www.iwm.org.uk/collections. In addition to Collections Online, you can visit the Visitor Rooms where you can explore over 8 million photographs, thousands of hours of moving images, the largest sound archive of its kind in the world, thousands of diaries and letters written by people in wartime, and a huge reference library. To make an appointment, call (020) 7416 5320, or e-mail mail@iwm.org.uk
Imperial War Museums www.iwm.org.uk

Front Cover: Art by Graham Turner, © Osprey Publishing
Back Cover: Photo courtesy NARA

Osprey Publishing supports the Woodland Trust, the UK's leading woodland conservation charity. Between 2014 and 2018 our donations are being spent on their Centenary Woods project in the UK.

To find out more about our authors and books visit www.ospreypublishing.com. Here you will find extracts, author interviews, details of forthcoming events and the option to sign up for our newsletter.

Author's Acknowledgements
This, the first-ever English-language account of the 'Battle of Britain' written from the Luftwaffe's operational perspective, is the product of the synergistic efforts of several individuals. First and foremost, I must praise editor Tom Milner for his vision of – and determination to see to fruition – Osprey's new Air Campaign series and I thank him for the privilege of allowing me to write the premier volume of this new series, fittingly on history's prototypical independent air campaign. I am also deeply indebted to Paul E. Eden, the noted British aviation historian, journalist and editor – who first recommended an air campaign series to Osprey years ago – for his unstinting encouragement and steadfast support of my efforts in this project. His excellent, insightful critique and thought-provoking questions made the final product far better than it ever could have been otherwise. Also to be thanked are fellow Osprey authors Chris Goss, Paul Crickmore and Ryan Noppen for their astute feedback and generous suggestions. I thank, too, Ms. Gina McNeely, whose tireless research at the US National Archive and Records Administration (NARA) provided numerous World War II Luftwaffe photographs from 1940, several of which are published herein for the first time. Finally, and most importantly, I thank my dear wife, Ann, for her incredible inspiration in her continuing – and thus far victorious – battle with a life-threatening disease and her constant wellspring of strength, patience, and motivation in completing this project. I have long wanted to research, comprehend, evaluate, and describe in detail the 'Battle of Britain' from the air campaign – in this case, the Luftwaffe's – perspective, and these are the people who have enabled and encouraged me to do so – to each one I say simply, but profoundly, 'Thank you.'

Contents

INTRODUCTION

Origins of the campaign

'Was nun?' ('What now?') In June 1940, when the panzers reached the Channel coast and the conquest of France was complete, the Wehrmacht had no plans or preparations for a cross-Channel invasion of Britain. (NARA)

The epic clash of air forces over southern England during the late summer and autumn of 1940 – that fierce aerial struggle we know today as 'The Battle of Britain' – was, in fact, both the goal and the culmination of Adolf Hitler's *Westfeldzug* ('Western Campaign'), which began on 10 May 1940 as the invasion of France and the Low Countries. Following a series of successful *Blumenkriege* ('flower wars') – five bloodless victories[1] that progressively stunned the peaceful peoples and political leadership of Britain and France – Hitler started World War II with a full-blown invasion of the 20-year-old nation of Poland. Having allowed the previous episodes to pass with no more than hollow rhetoric and worthless accords – due almost entirely to the Allies' woeful unpreparedness for war, especially in terms of their air forces – on 25 August the governments of Britain and France pledged that if Hitler invaded Poland, they would declare war on Germany. Undeterred, Hitler launched *Fall Weiß* ('Case White') on 1 September, and three days later Germany, for the second time in 25 years, was once again at war with the two western democracies.

The real aim of Hitler's unrelenting succession of territorial acquisitions and conquests – espoused in the second volume of his polemic manifesto *Mein Kampf* and his bellicose rhetoric once in power – was the invasion of Soviet Russia and the elimination of Bolshevik Communism as a threat to Nazi Germany. To avoid the Kaiser's most egregious strategic error of World War I – the ill-fated attempt to fight a 'two-front war' – Hitler had adroitly, and at least temporarily, neutralized the threat from the East with the 23 August 1939 signing of the Molotov-Ribbentrop Pact that divided Poland between Germany and the Soviet Union (USSR). The pact's pledges of non-aggression between the two not only gave Hitler time to prepare for the pursuit of his ultimate geopolitical goal – the invasion of

---

1 These were: occupation of the Rhineland in March 1936, annexation of Austria in April 1938, occupation of the Sudetenland in October 1938, the occupation of the rest of Bohemia-Moravia and the annexation of Lithuania's Memel district in March 1939.

Russia – but also conveniently provided an effective preventative to keep Soviet Premier Josef Stalin from intervening in, or joining in, a war in the West.

In fact, the chief reason for the Wehrmacht ('armed forces') leadership's continued support of *der Führer* was that he had effectively eliminated the threat of having to fight a 'two-front war'. However, the Allies' seemingly hasty, imprudent and ineffective declaration of war now dictated that France and Britain must be eliminated from the conflict before it could be continued against Soviet Russia. Consequently, on 9 October 1939, even before the embers of a heavily bombed and burnt-out Warsaw had cooled, Hitler directed his military chiefs to begin planning *Fall Gelb* ('Case Yellow' – the deployment order for the invasion of France), a pre-emptive offensive campaign 'on the northern flank of the Western front, through Luxembourg, Belgium and Holland.'

While France could be – and was – conquered by the army's revolutionary *blitzkrieg* ('lightning war') mechanized air-land campaign,[2] in all pre-war planning German army and navy leaders readily

Nazi dictator Adolf Hitler with OKH chief *Generaloberst* Walther von Brauchitsch at Warsaw in October 1939. Before he could continue his quest to destroy Communist Russia, Hitler had to 'knock England out of the war'. Because of British intransigence, it appeared that invading England was the only solution. (Bundesarchiv Bild 183-2001-0706-501, Photographer Mensing)

recognized that the Wehrmacht's otherwise powerful 'war machine' completely lacked the means to launch an amphibious offensive against the British Isles. Consequently, such an operation was neither considered nor planned before the panzers arrived at the Channel coast in June 1940. In fact, at that time the Wehrmacht's strategic planning for defeating Britain lay in the hope of an effective U-boat blockade (called *Handelskrieg* or 'trade warfare') and a strategic air offensive against British ports, armaments industries, and oil refinery and storage facilities. Consequently, Hitler's stated purpose, ordered by his 'War Directive No. 6', was for the *Fall Gelb* offensive 'to win as much territory as possible in Holland, Belgium, and Northern France, to serve as a base for the successful prosecution of the air and sea war against England.'

Since signing the Anglo-German Naval Agreement in June 1935, Germany's *Kriegsmarine* ('War Navy') had concentrated on an ambitious – and exceedingly expensive and time consuming – capital ship construction programme, and as a result the sea service had only 27 ocean-going submarines (of 57 total) when Hitler invaded Poland. Encouraged by the fairly effective – but not decisive – U-boat campaign during World War I, Germany's inferiority to the Royal Navy (RN) in capital ships quickly caused *Großadmiral* (Grand Admiral) Erich Raeder to realign his navy's priorities and begin building increased numbers of the much cheaper and more speedily produced submarines. However, peacetime construction rates (one per month) continued until greater quantities of steel arrived in June when the rate increased to four per month. Although during the first nine months of the war, the U-boats sank 261 merchantmen (nearly 1 million gross registered tons) and had spectacular successes against RN units, such as sinking the battleship HMS *Royal Oak*

2 See Osprey Campaigns 264 and 265: *Fall Gelb 1940*, Vols 1 and 2, by this author.

U-boat leaving on patrol. When the French capitulated, leaving Britain alone to fight Nazi Germany, the *Kriegsmarine* had only 15 operational ocean-going U-boats, insufficient to mount the submarine blockade envisioned by Hitler and his Wehrmacht planners, at least until the spring of 1941. (NARA)

in Scapa Flow and the aircraft carrier HMS *Courageous* while on anti-submarine patrol, the Kriegsmarine was actually losing the initial phase of what became known as the 'Battle of the Atlantic', with 24 U-boats being lost by June 1940. Since it took nine months to train replacement crews, the laggardly construction and time-consuming training programmes could not keep pace with losses. Consequently, in June 1940 the Kriegsmarine had only 15 ocean-going and 18 coastal U-boats (plus seven training subs). Until construction and training outpaced losses by a wide margin, Raeder had little hope of mounting an effective, economy-strangling submarine blockade for at least another year.

Therefore, only the newest of Germany's military services – the Luftwaffe – could effectively carry the war to the British in the short term. Having begun as a small office within the Weimar Republic's *Truppenamt* ('Army Troop Bureau'), supervising a handful of clandestine flying units and a training establishment at Lipetsk in the USSR, the Luftwaffe had from the start embraced 'strategic air warfare' as one of its three combat missions. The first opportunity to plan to employ the Luftwaffe in this revolutionary role was in August–September 1938 when Hitler made the first bellicose moves to subjugate Czechoslovakia. His deputy, *Reichsluftminister* (National Aviation Minister) and self-appointed commander-in-chief of the Luftwaffe, Hermann Göring, feared a strong British reaction – most notably by Royal Air Force (RAF) Bomber Command – and directed *General der Flieger* Hellmuth Felmy, commander of what would soon become *Luftflotte* ('Air Fleet') 2, to provide an assessment of his command's counter-offensive potential.

Felmy's *Planstudie 38* determined: 'A war of annihilation against England appears to be out of the question with the resources thus far available,' because most industrial targets lay beyond the range of his medium bombers, the meagre size of his bomber force was limited by the lack of modern airfields, and there were no escort fighters yet available. Felmy's conclusion was that 'the only solution… [is] to seize bases in the Low Countries [Holland and Belgium] before undertaking an air offensive against the British.'

Real planning began the next year with an intelligence report by *Major* Josef Schmid. An ambitious non-flying officer, Schmid was a close associate of Göring's who made his mark on the *Oberkommando der Luftwaffe* (ObdL; 'Luftwaffe headquarters' or HQ) leadership by producing three glowingly optimistic intelligence assessments in early 1939.[3] Using information from the Luftwaffe's air attaché in London, the *Abwehr*[4] espionage network, *Generalmajor* Wolfgang Martini's radio monitoring service, and photographs from *Oberst*

---

3 These were *Studie Blau* (blue: Britain), *Studie Grün* (green: Poland) and *Studie Rot* (red: France).

4 The Abwehr was the OKW's intelligence bureau: Amt Ausland/Abwehr im OKW, or 'Foreign Affairs/Defence Bureau of the Armed Forces High Command.'

(Colonel) Theodor Rowehl's clandestine photo-reconnaissance unit using camera-equipped He 111C 'mailplanes' flying Lufthansa 'route proving trials', Schmid assembled a collection of data into a coherent – but not completely accurate – intelligence assessment codenamed *Studie Blau* ('Study Blue').

A preliminary report was published on 2 May 1939 and sent to Göring and three Luftflotte commanders. Schmid warned that RAF fighter strength was projected to match the *Jagdwaffe* ('fighter forces') by 1941 but that current 'British defences [were] inadequate to defend anything more than the general areas around London. This would leave the rest of England open to attack.' Through Martini's service, Schmid and the Luftwaffe leadership were made aware of the RAF's new early warning radar network, but no one recognized its capabilities or its potential, and Schmid did not mention it in his report.

Felmy disagreed with Schmid's assessment and on 13 May countered by issuing Luftflotte 2's *Studieplan 39*, which resulted from a five-day staff exercise witnessed by the Luftwaffe's new chief of staff (COS), *Generalmajor* Hans Jeschonnek, and the COSs from the other two air fleets. In it Felmy reiterated that a successful long-range strategic air campaign against British industries was doubtful, even using projected 1942 equipment/force structure.

Jeschonnek returned to ObdL and, once his operations staff had reviewed both studies, published a final appraisal on 22 May, deciding that a strategic air campaign was not possible because 'the [British] western and southern ports lay beyond the range of Luftflotte 2,' and added 'furthermore, terror attacks on London as the stronghold of the enemy defence would hardly have a catastrophic effect or contribute significantly to a war decision.' With this guidance and the target list provided by *Studie Blau*, on 9 July 1939, ObdL issued instructions to begin developing an air attack plan against British war industries and supply centres once closer bases, or longer-range bombers, were acquired.

Four months later, anticipating a favourable outcome to the *Fall Gelb* offensive – which was being repeatedly postponed due to chronically inclement weather – on 29 November 1939, Hitler had his personal military staff (OKW – *Oberkommando der Wehrmacht*, 'High Command of the Armed Forces') issue War Directive No. 9, 'Instructions for warfare against the economy of the enemy' stating, 'Should the Army succeed in defeating the Anglo-French Armies in the field and in seizing and holding a sector of the coast of the Continent opposite England, the task of the Navy and Air Force to carry the war to English industry becomes paramount.'

CHRONOLOGY

1938

22 September First Luftwaffe operations (Luftwaffengruppenkommando 2) staff study on possible air offensive against Great Britain completed. Conclusion: 'seize bases in [Holland and Belgium] before undertaking an air offensive against the British'.

1939

22 May *Studie Blau* – the Luftwaffe HQ's first detailed staff study regarding possible air offensive against Great Britain – is briefed to Göring and Luftwaffe leadership, becoming a basis for future planning.

1 September Germany invades Poland, starting World War II.

3 September Britain and France declare war on Germany.

9 October OKW issues Hitler's 'War Directive No. 6', ordering OKH (*Oberkommando des Heeres*, 'High Command of the Army') to begin planning the invasion of northern France and the Low Countries to capture territory for a Luftwaffe and U-boat offensive against Britain.

November OKH and OKM (*Oberkommando der Marine*, 'Naval High Command') staff studies explore the possibility of landing troops in England – both reach negative conclusions.

22 November Luftwaffe Intelligence office produces *Proposal for the Conduct of Air Warfare against Britain*, a conceptual strategic air offensive targeting plan, based largely on *Studie Blau*.

29 November OKW issues Hitler's 'War Directive No. 9, Conduct of the War against the economy of the enemy', authorizing Luftwaffe to begin bombing British ports, depots, oil and food storage, and industrial plants once suitable airfields were captured in northern France, Belgium and Holland.

1940

9 April Operation *Weserübung* ('*Weser Exercise*') begins, occupying Denmark and Norway.

10 May *Fall Gelb* campaign begins, overrunning Holland, Belgium and northern France.

15 May Dutch Army surrenders.

24 May OKW issues Hitler's 'War Directive No. 13', authorizing the Luftwaffe 'to attack the English homeland in the fullest manner, as soon as sufficient forces are available… in accordance with principles laid down in Directive No. 9'.

28 May Belgian Army surrenders.

22 June France signs Armistice with Germany.

25 June Hitler directs OKW Operations Staff to prepare a 'basic study for an invasion of England'.

30 June Göring issues ObdL Directive to commanders of Luftflotten 2, 3, and 5 for the conduct of offensive operations against Great Britain, implementing Hitler/OKW Directive No. 13.

2 July OKW chief *Generaloberst* Wilhelm Keitel directs the three armed services to provide OKW with basic proposals, including force requirements and timing estimates, for a cross-Channel amphibious operation to invade Britain.

2 July–11 August Preliminary phase of 'Battle of Britain' – *Kanalkampf* ('Channel Battle'), operations initially conducted under the guidance of Hitler's 'War Directive No. 9'.

11 July OKM chief *Großadmiral* (Grand Admiral) Erich Raeder meets with Hitler to discourage consideration of a cross-Channel operation in the immediate future, at least until 'complete air superiority' is assured. Hitler decides to continue planning for the operation anyway.

12 July OKW COS Alfred Jodl promulgates first memorandum outlining concept of cross-Channel operation, tentatively named *Unternehmen Löwe* (Operation *Lion*).

13 July Hitler meets with OKH leadership, which briefs him on the army's requirements for a cross-Channel operation.

16 July OKW issues Hitler's Directive No. 16, 'On Preparations for a Landing Operation against

England' directing services to provide detailed planning requirements and concepts of operations (CONOPS).

18–21 July Göring holds the first staff conference to discuss implementing Directive No. 16. Two days later, he hosts a victory (over France) celebration for senior Luftwaffe officers and the next day confers with the three Luftflotten commanders to discuss attacking British fleet units and bases.

21 July First 'joint conference' for planning Operation *Seelöwe* ('*Sea Lion*'); Hitler meets with OKH chief *Generaloberst* Walther von Brauchitsch, Raeder, and Jeschonnek. Recognizing the vast differences in the OKH and OKM proposals, Hitler orders a conference for 29–31 July to determine a consolidated joint CONOPS.

24 July–1 August 'Commanders' Assessments' memoranda exchanged between ObdL and Luftflotten and Fliegerkorps HQs outline objectives, priorities, and proposed CONOPS for an offensive counter-air campaign (OCA) against the RAF.

1 August OKW issues Hitler's War Directive No. 17, 'Conduct of Air and Sea Warfare against Britain', ordering the Luftwaffe to 'overpower the English air force with all the forces at its command, in the shortest possible time… in order to establish the necessary conditions [air superiority] for the final conquest of England.'

2 August Following conference the previous day in The Hague with Luftflotten commanders and senior staff officers, Göring issues 'Preparations and Directives for "Operation Eagle"', concentrating attacks on RAF installations and aviation industries, with the RN as the second priority.

6 August Last ObdL 'pre-operational conference'; Luftwaffe preparations complete but bad weather precludes large-scale operations for five days.

12 August *Adlerangriff* ('Eagle Attack') begins with preliminary bombardment of six RAF radar stations and three coastal fighter airfields.

13 August *Adlertag* ('Eagle Day') officially begins the Luftwaffe's OCA campaign against the RAF.

12–18 August *Adlerangriff* Phase I: attacks primarily against RAF in general, with secondary attacks against RN facilities and ports.

16 August OKW Directive sets 15 September as 'A-Day' for Operation *Seelöwe* (Sea Lion).

24 August–6 September *Adlerangriff* Phase II: attacks concentrated against RAF Fighter Command No. 11 Group sector stations and fighter airfields.

24/25 August Accidental night bombing of London.

25/26 August RAF reprisal bombing attempt against Berlin.

30 August Hitler authorizes bombing of London in retaliation for RAF attempts at bombing Berlin. Final Operation *Seelöwe* plan issued by OKH.

3 September OKW order establishes timetable for *Seelöwe* with S-Tag (German 'D-Day') set for 21 September.

5/6 September Luftwaffe's first intentional bombing of London.

6 September ObdL discusses and determines new tactics – attacking London in the hopes of drawing Fighter Command into battle – for Phase III.

7–30 September *Adlerangriff* Phase III: attacks concentrated against London in effort to draw Fighter Command into battle of attrition in fighter-vs-fighter combat.

14 September Hitler postpones initiating *Seelöwe* to 17 September, pushing S-Tag back to 26 September.

15 September The climactic battle of the campaign, now remembered as 'Battle of Britain Day' in the UK.

17 September With air superiority not achieved; Hitler postpones *Seelöwe* indefinitely, essentially cancelling the proposed invasion of Great Britain, and signalling the Luftwaffe's defeat.

30 September Luftwaffe's last major daylight attack on London.

29 October Luftwaffe's last major daylight bombing mission on England.

ATTACKER'S CAPABILITIES
The Luftwaffe

Doctrine: strategic attack and tactical support

When Hitler officially unveiled the Luftwaffe in March 1935, it came complete with an air power doctrine whose formulation had begun almost ten years earlier, in the secrecy of the Reichswehr's *Truppenamt Luftschutzreferat* ('Army Troop Bureau, Air Defence Desk', abbreviated TA [L]). Entitled *Richtlinien für die Führungs des operative Luftkrieges* ('Directives for the Conduct of the Operational Air War') and published in May 1926, this document became the guidance for organization, targeting strategy, and operational parameters for the nascent Luftwaffe and its wartime roles. In addition to protection of important government and industrial sites, two primary missions were envisioned: those flown by a 'tactical air force' oriented towards supporting the army and navy and those conducted by a 'strategic air force' organized for the destruction of targets in the enemy homeland.

Authored by *Oberstleutnant* (Lieutenant Colonel) Helmuth Wilberg and his three-man 'air staff', the Directives postulated that the 'strategic air force' might have a decisive effect in demoralizing the enemy population (a notion popularized by Italian air power theorist Giulio Douhet) and by damaging the enemy's armaments industries, electricity generating systems, transportation networks, and port facilities. The 'strategic bomber divisions' would be equipped with long-range heavy bombers – able to reach the USSR's Ural Mountains, or the UK's northern Scottish coast (i.e. the naval base at Scapa Flow) from bases within Germany – as well as strategic reconnaissance aircraft and long-range, heavily armed, two-seat escort fighters to enable the bomber formations to penetrate enemy air defences. Because of their inherent range capability, these units were seen as the only force capable of attacking the enemy homeland from the very outset of hostilities, yet they could also support a ground or maritime offensive by bombing enemy transportation nets, seaports and naval bases.

In 1934 Wilberg, now a major general, was appointed by the Luftwaffe COS, *Generalleutnant* (Lieutenant General) Walter Wever, to codify the service's operational air doctrine, which was published the following year as *Luftwaffe Dienstvorschrift 16:*

Luftkriegführung (Luftwaffe Service Regulation 16: Air War Guidance, or LDv 16). The eight-year evolution of the Luftwaffe's offensive doctrine had eschewed its earlier Douhetian notions, saying, 'Attacks against cities made for the purpose of inducing terror in the civilian populace are to be avoided on principle.' Instead, the published guidance identified the primary mission of the Luftwaffe as 'the attack on the sources of enemy power.' These included armaments industries, food production, import facilities, power stations, railway networks, military installations, and government administrative centres.

Aircraft development

During this secret, formative period, the development of German military aviation closely paralleled the Luftwaffe's doctrinal guidance. Responding to Wilberg's initial treatise and taking advantage of the increased latitude permitted by the May 1926 'Paris Agreement' that relaxed some aerial aspects of the Versailles Peace Treaty, the air officer in the Reichswehr's Heereswaffenamt ('Army Weapons Bureau') – *Hauptmann* (Captain) Kurt Student – issued invitations to surviving German aircraft manufacturers to submit designs for four types of military aircraft. After testing at Lipetsk in 1930–33, these became the Luftwaffe's first generation of combat aircraft: the Arado Ar 64/65 and Heinkel He 51 biplane fighters, the He 45/46 army reconnaissance aircraft, and the two-seat Junkers K 47 'night fighter-reconnaissance' (which led directly to the He 50 biplane dive-bomber) aeroplane. The requirement for a 'long-range, middle altitude reconnaissance' (at the time, a euphemism for *Grossnachtbomber* or 'large night bomber') aircraft – which specified a four-engine type with a speed of 133mph (215km/h) and altitude of 16,500ft (5,000m) – could not be met with existing technologies and no designs were tendered by any manufacturer.

The second round of aircraft requirements was issued in the summer of 1932, just as the first generation of combat aircraft was being introduced into the newly formed 22-*staffel* (squadron) Reichsluftwaffe. Five types were required: a single-seat 'light fighter' which became the Messerschmitt Bf 109; a two-seat 'heavy fighter' which became the Bf 110; a 'heavy dive bomber', the Junkers Ju 87 'Stuka'; a fast, twin-engine medium bomber, the He 111, for tactical strikes; and a four-engine heavy bomber for strategic attack. The requirements for the latter were for an aircraft to carry 1,100kg (2,425lb) of bombs a distance of 2,500km (1,553 miles), later revised to 1,600kg (3,527lb) of bombs for 2,000km (1,243 miles).

Given first priority for development, four years later two prototype four-engine, long-range, heavy bombers, the Dornier Do 19 and Junkers Ju 89, were received for testing. First flown on 28 October 1936, the Do 19 V1 prototype was powered by four 715hp Bramo 322 H-2 radials but could only manage a top speed of 197mph (315km/h) empty and without its defensive armament. Flying two months later, the Ju 89 V1 was powered by four 1,075hp Jumo 211 A inline engines and was 45mph (72km/h) faster, but was still considered too slow. Both bombers carried a crew of nine and had identical defensive arrangements: two 7.92mm MG 15 machine guns in the nose and tail and two 20mm cannon mounted in dorsal and ventral turrets. Without the power-boosting superchargers that made the contemporary Boeing B-17A (and onwards) a success, the so-called 'Ural Bombers' proved to be chronically underpowered and could not achieve their required performance specifications.

The Do 19 'Ural Bomber' was developed in the mid-1930s as Germany's first attempt to produce a long-range, four-engine bomber – its failure resulted in a six-year delay in the Luftwaffe obtaining a heavy bomber. (NMUSAF)

Junkers Ju 89 'Ural Bomber' V1 prototype in flight in 1937. Although more promising than the Do 19, its performance was still inadequate and its cost was considered prohibitive. The two prototypes were converted into long-ranged transports and used in the Norwegian campaign in 1940. (Bundesarchiv Bild 141-2409; photographer unknown)

Wever was disappointed in both designs and, even before their first flights – just prior to his death in a crash in June 1936 – he ordered a new study called 'Bomber A'. This project eventually resulted in the problem-plagued Heinkel He 177 heavy bomber. It was planned to be operational by mid-1942, with a force of 500 bombers (of 703 ordered) available by 1 April the following year.

With the arrival of the 660-mile (1,065km) range He 111, on 29 April 1937 *Generalleutnant* Albert Kesselring (Wever's replacement) decided that Germany could not afford to spend twice the resources – twice as many engines, double the fuel consumption, and 2.5 times the aluminium – for roughly the same bomb-load, so he accepted the shorter-ranged medium bomber, which he concluded could perform both strategic and tactical bombing, to a maximum of 500km (300 miles) beyond Germany's borders or the battlefront. Kesselring had the full agreement of *Generaloberst* (Colonel General) Hermann Göring, the corpulent, vainglorious leader of the Luftwaffe, who is quoted as saying, '*Der Führer* will never ask me how big our bombers are, but how many we have.'

Whether powered by two engines or four, bombers dominated the Reichluftwaffe's force structure planning. The May 1933 expansion to 45 squadrons was to field 27 bomber squadrons (including five auxiliary bomber/transport units), 12 reconnaissance squadrons (half corps-level/half long-range), and six *Jagdstaffeln* ('fighter squadrons' – three each heavy and light) to be achieved by 1 October 1935. Consisting of 600 combat aircraft stationed at 36 fully equipped air bases, at this visionary stage the organization of these forces was still rather notional, but their intended roles – strategic and tactical – and their missions were well understood. Under the nascent air service's developing doctrine, fast, twin-engine medium bombers would penetrate into enemy territory, striking targets 30 to 300 miles beyond the national borders or battlefront. Due to inaccuracies inherent to early bombing technologies, they were best used against large area targets, such as barracks, troop concentrations, military vehicle parks, and motorized or marching columns, all focusing on disrupting enemy reinforcements from reaching the front lines. Deeper, they would attack railway stations and marshalling yards, fuel storage and stockpiles of equipment, and port facilities to interdict the flow of men, equipment and supplies towards the front.

Whether strategic or tactical, it was fundamental to the developing employment doctrine that the first step – and the prerequisite for further air or ground operations – was the elimination of the enemy's air force, or to so reduce its combat strength as to render it ineffective. Achieving *Luftüberlegenheit* ('air superiority') over enemy territory required attacking the enemy's aircraft where they were most vulnerable – on the ground – in the opening moments of the offensive and continuing attacks on air bases and depots, and even against enemy aviation industries, especially aero engine manufacturers, that could provide replacements for losses sustained in the opening rounds. Today this is known as an 'offensive counter-air' (OCA) campaign and became the Luftwaffe's textbook opening move in all of the eight invasions that Hitler would launch against other European nations within the next six years.

When *Generalleutnant* Albert Kesselring faced the Luftwaffe's economic realities, he was forced to decide that Germany's limited resources were better invested in twice as many medium bombers than in limited numbers of four-engine bombers carrying about the same amount of bombs. (NARA)

Capabilities, roles, and missions

When the Luftwaffe was unveiled, the embryonic air arm had six squadrons of awkward and inadequate Dornier Do 11/23 twin-engine bombers and seven equipped with Junkers Ju 52/3m trimotor bomber/transports, all slated to be replaced with two modern, twin-engine bomber designs. In February 1937, the first squadrons of the new, purpose-designed, twin-engine He 111B medium bomber and the Do 17E twin-engine mailplane-cum-light bomber joined the Luftwaffe's bomber force, allowing the long-sought expansion to finally begin.

The 1933 expansion plan proved grossly over-optimistic, with staff studies quickly concluding that the German aviation industry – initially based on four airframe and four

The Heinkel He 111 was the Luftwaffe's first purpose-designed, modern twin-engine medium bomber. The 'pod' mounted beneath the nose contained the ineffective Lofte 7 bombsight and the bombs were loaded vertically, nose up to prevent setting off the detonator, in 'bins' in the belly. (Bundesarchiv Bild 183-C0214-0007-013; photographer unknown)

engine manufacturers – could not hope to provide 600 new warplanes in two and a half years. To make matters worse, ten months after Hitler, Göring, and the Nazis came to power (on 3 February 1933) they ordered the Luftwaffe's expansion increased to 2,000 aircraft! Fortunately, there was one civil aviation contract already in place that would help meet that goal. In 1932, the Heereswaffenamt, which controlled development of all commercial as well as military aircraft, issued a specification for a high-speed mailplane and six-passenger executive transport for *Deutsche Luft Hansa A.G.* (DLH), the German national airline, and a light freight transport for *Deutsche Reichsbahn-Gesellschaft*, the German national railways. Design work began in August that year and on 23 March the next year, in one of his first official acts, Göring's deputy, Erhard Milch, the former director of DLH, authorized construction of prototypes. Because of his previous World War I and DLH experience,

Using dive-bombing to obtain more accurate weapons deliveries, the new Ju 87A 'Stuka' became an effective tactical close air support aircraft, provided it was operated in a 'permissive' (i.e., air superiority achieved) environment. (NMUSAF)

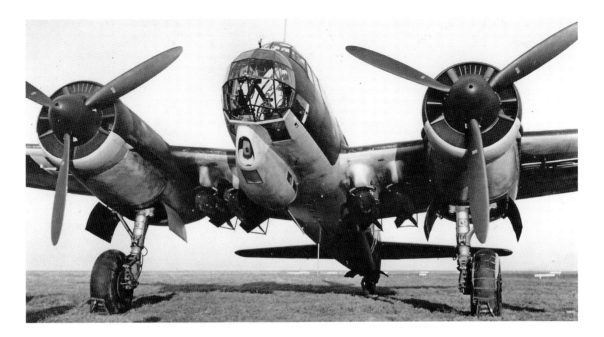

Milch was well aware that the Do 17 mailplane had potential as a high speed twin-engine light bomber and, in the prototype contract, he specified that 'even the civil version should be capable of rapid conversion to a military role.' Powered by a pair of 750hp BMW VI in-line engines, the resulting Do 17E could only carry two 250kg (550lb) or eight 50kg (220lb) bombs, but it did so at 220mph (355km/hr), 15mph (24km/hr) faster than contemporary British and French fighters. The ultimate version of the type – appropriately suffixed 'Z' – was upgraded using 1,000hp Bramo Fafnir 323P radials, enabling it to carry 1,000kg (2,205lb) of bombs. Specializing in low-altitude level deliveries to ensure greater accuracy against smaller targets, the Do 17Z was primarily used for relatively short-ranged 'battlefield interdiction' and airfield attacks. By July 1940, the Dornier equipped eight *Kampfgruppen* ('bomber groups'), although – considered obsolescent – these were slated for re-equipment with the new third-generation Ju 88A 'Wonderbomber'.

Fielded almost simultaneously was the purpose-designed twin-engine medium bomber, the He 111. Intended for deeper interdiction (railways, seaports, other logistics choke points) as well as strategic bombardment, the definitive He 111H/P (suffix dependent upon the engine type used) could carry 4,410lb (2,000kg) of bombs and had an effective combat radius of 300 miles (483km). This could be extended to 400 miles (645km), but only by reducing the bomb-load to a paltry 1,100lb (500kg). In any event, this distance was well beyond the range of any available fighter escort, which was required because the He 111 was inadequately defended, having only two flexible 7.92mm Rheinmetall MG 15 machine guns in the rear-facing dorsal and ventral positions and a third in the nose. Although losses to RAF fighters would soon result in additional weapons being mounted (in rather awkward positions), the only real antidote was effective fighter escort. In July 1940, the Heinkel was the Luftwaffe's standard medium bomber, equipping 15 of the 33 *Kampfgruppen* gathered along the Channel coast for the Battle of Britain.

Typically, in order to reduce exposure to anti-aircraft (AA) fire, the He 111s bombed from 4,000m (13,123ft). However, from this altitude the Zeiss *Lotfernrohr* 3 ('vertical telescope') bombsight did not permit accurate bombing. In fact, for both the Dornier and Heinkel, in tests in 1937, their bomb-aimers were able to place only two per cent of their bombs within a 200m (660ft) radius around the target. The lack of accuracy inherent in medium-altitude level deliveries led directly to the Luftwaffe's obsession with 'dive-bombing', especially for

The Luftwaffe's third-generation medium bomber was the Junkers Ju 88A, which effectively merged the bombing payload of a twin-engine bomber with the accuracy of a dive bomber. (IWM MH 7517)

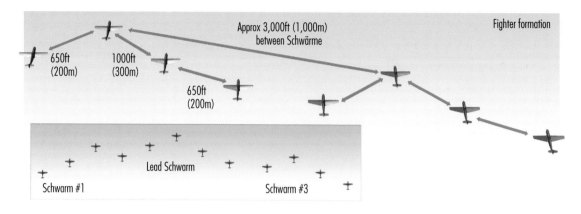

Fighter formation

Approx 3,000ft (1,000m) between Schwärme

650ft (200m)

1000ft (300m)

650ft (200m)

Lead Schwarm

Schwarm #1

Schwarm #3

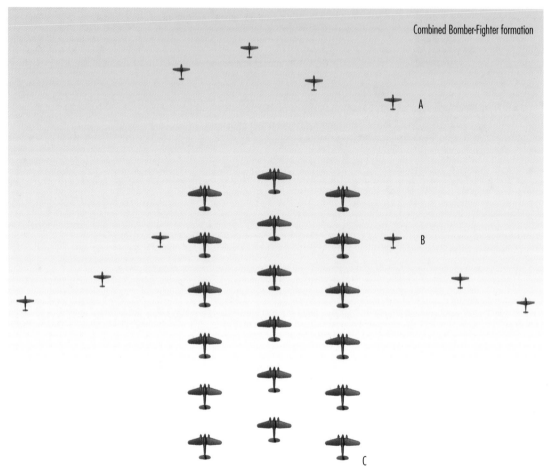

Combined Bomber-Fighter formation

A

B

C

Key

A. One Jagdgruppe sweeps ('freie Jagd') ahead of the bomber formation. Typically led by Jagdgeschwader commander and his Geschwaderstab ('staff') flight.

B. The other two Jagdgruppen provide Jagdschutz ('fighter protection' or close escort) by flying alongside the bomber formation and protecting its flanks.

C. Kampgeschwader bomber formation.

OPPOSITE LUFTWAFFE COMBAT FORMATIONS

The standard Luftwaffe fighter formation was a four-aeroplane *Schwarm* composed of two pairs (*Rotte*) operating as one flight. The two wingmen (on the flanks) flew approximately 200m alongside and slightly aft of their *Rottenführer* ('two-ship leader') with the second Rottenführer flying 300m alongside and aft of the *Schwarmführer* ('four-ship leader'). In both pair the leaders could engage enemy aircraft, co-ordinating their attacks via radio, while each *Katschmarek* ('wingman') protected his leader's tail.

Typically a nine-aeroplane (plus one to three reserves) Jagdstaffel would launch two Schwärme but were frequently augmented by the group *Stabsschwarm* ('staff flight'), so that three Schwärme – 12 fighters – could be flown in the near line abreast *freie Jagd* ('free hunting' or 'fighter sweep') formation shown in the inset.

Messerschmitt Bf 110C *Zerstörer* 'heavy fighter' was intended as the bomber escort for deep penetration bombing missions. However, no one considered the outcome of it engaging defending interceptors. (NMUSAF)

pinpoint attacks against small targets such as bunkers, bridges, artillery emplacements, field HQs, and communications sites. Following successful trials with the He 50 biplane first-generation dive-bomber, the Luftwaffe ordered the large, robust Ju 87 'Stuka' (short for *Sturzkampfflugzeug* or 'dive-bombing aeroplane') as its primary tactical support aircraft. Terminally slow due to its heavy weight and fixed, spatted undercarriage, and poorly defended by a single flexible MG 15 facing aft, the type required a permissive environment – i.e., air superiority – in order to do its job without prohibitive losses.

Mating the best attributes of both types of bombing attacks was the new, third-generation Ju 88 – a fast, twin-engine medium bomber with dive-bombing capability, the prototype of which first flew in December 1936. Powered by a pair of 1,200hp Jumo 211B in-line engines, the Ju 88A could carry a 5,291lb (2,400kg) bomb-load a distance of 782 miles (1,260km), giving it an effective combat radius of 360 miles. While its demonstrated top speed (empty at 18,050ft/5,500m) was 280mph (450km/h), the *Schnellbomber* ('fast bomber') typically cruised at 217–230mph and was defended by two dorsal and a third ventral MG 15s. The type was initially issued to I./KG 30 – a unit specializing in anti-shipping attacks – which flew its first mission on 26 September 1939. By July the next year a sweeping re-equipment programme was under way, with three *Kampfgruppen* (KG 77) undergoing conversion to the new type in Germany, while ten Ju 88 groups were on the front line along the Channel coast.

It was fundamental to Luftwaffe employment doctrine that fighter escorts were needed to get the bombers to their targets. This requirement resulted in the long-range Messerschmitt Bf 110 *Kampfzerstörer* ('battle destroyer') heavy fighter, which first flew on 12 May 1936. A slim, fast, twin-engine two-seater, the *Zerstörer* mounted a nose battery of two 20mm cannon and four 7.92mm machine guns, and was intended to range ahead of the bombers and sweep away enemy interceptors before them, as well as provide close escort for the He 111s and Do 17s. What was not appreciated was that the 'destroyer's' adversaries, being

The superb Messerschmitt Bf 109B single-seat 'frontal fighter' was designed to achieve aerial superiority over the front lines, to a depth of 30 miles beyond, and provide air defence for the Third Reich's vital industrial centres. (NMUSAF)

primarily small, light interceptors, would have a decisive manoeuvring advantage once combat was joined.

The doctrinal requirement for fighter escorts was so well accepted that the Luftwaffe's initial procurement and force structure plans intended for half of the *Jagdwaffe* to be heavy fighters. However, the Bf 110's development lagged while the Bf 109 was improved quickly through four iterations, resulting in the superb Bf 109E 'Emil'. When Hitler began World War II by invading Poland, seven of ten *Zerstörergruppen* ('destroyer groups') in the Luftwaffe's order of battle were actually equipped with the Bf 109D as interim equipment.

The *Zerstörer's* likely adversaries were not unlike the Luftwaffe's own defensive 'light fighter', the Messerschmitt Bf 109, first flown on 28 May 1935. A sleek, fast, single-seater, the Bf 109 was designed as a quick-climbing bomber interceptor, initially mounting two 7.92mm MG 17 machine guns, later carrying four MG 17s or two MG 17s and a pair of MG FF 20mm cannon. Sacrificing, to a degree, some of the manoeuvrability traditional to fighters, the Bf 109's high performance meant that it could attack swiftly and disengage easily, at its pilot's discretion, obviating the need to outmanoeuvre an opponent in a dogfight. Planned as a frontal defensive fighter – assuming the mantle of 1918's Fokker D.VII – and point defence interceptor, doctrinally it was intended to provide air superiority over the front lines, to a depth of approximately 50km (30 miles), as well as defending vital industrial and political centres within Germany. Consequently, the thought of extending the type's limited range/endurance through the use of jettisonable external fuel tanks only occurred to the Luftwaffe's leadership after battle over England was joined. The Bf 109E-7 was equipped to carry a 300-litre (66 Imp gal) moulded plywood 'drop tank' – which doubled the fighter's operating radius – but these did not begin to arrive to the first frontline unit (I.(J)/LG 2) until August and the unit was not operational until the end of September. Retro-fitting earlier versions did not begin until October, after the campaign was over.

Finally, a word needs to be said about the Luftwaffe's reconnaissance units. That word is: inadequate. The service began Hitler's *Westfeldzug* with 17 *Aufklärungsstaffeln* ('reconnaissance squadrons'), four of which were gathered together in Aufklärungsgruppe ObdL (reconnaissance group for Luftwaffe HQ) based at airfields at Berlin and Oranienburg, and a fifth (1.(F)/124) was converting to the new Do 215 at Berlin-Templehof. Two others were based in Norway to reconnoitre the North Sea and northern Britain. The remaining ten squadrons had suffered heavy losses – 166 reconnaissance machines of all types – during the campaign and, at any one time, half were withdrawn from operations to regroup and train replacement aircrews. The rest found themselves tasked with the dual requirements of photographing RAF airfields and other OCA targets while simultaneously supporting the proposed cross-Channel assault with photo-reconnaissance missions covering coastal defences, potential landing beaches, and the railway network in southern England. Consequently, limited numbers of reconnaissance sorties were available to provide updated intelligence to the commanders of the two 'air fleets' (Luftflotten) that would be fighting over southern England.

Commanders

Two years after taking power and consolidating his personal and political grip on the German government, on 26 February 1935 Adolf Hitler signed the secret decree authorizing the establishment of the Luftwaffe (formerly the Reichsluftwaffe) as Germany's third military service, separate and independent from – and equal with – the Heer (army) and Kriegsmarine. In this decree, Hitler appointed **Hermann Wilhelm Göring** as commander-in-chief of the Luftwaffe. In doing so, Hitler was only ratifying the *de facto* command arrangements that had existed since 1933, when the Wehrmacht commander-in-chief and Minister of Defence, Nazi sympathizer *Generalfeldmarschall* (General Field Marshal) Werner von Blomberg, moved supervision of the nation's rather disparate secret military aviation activities – now consolidated in the *Luftschutz Amt* ('Air Defence Bureau' or *LS-amt*) office – from the Reichswehr staff to Göring's *Reichsluftfahrtministerium* (RLM or Reich Aviation Ministry) on 15 May 1933.

Hermann Göring in August 1932, wearing his *Pour le Mérite*. (NARA)

At this time the *LS-amt* was headed by *Oberst* Eberhardt Bohnstedt, said by Blomberg to be 'the stupidest clot I could find in my general staff'. On 1 September 1933, Bohnstedt was replaced by the former chief of training, *Oberst* Walther Wever, one of the 182 army officers transferred to 'flesh out' the new air service. To give Göring military authority over Wever, the day before, Blomberg reinstated Göring on the active officer rolls as a *General der Infanterie* (General of the Infantry).

As is well known, Göring had been a fighter pilot during World War I. Born to a Bavarian foreign service officer and his peasant wife in 1893, he attended the Berlin Lichterfelde military academy and joined the Imperial German army's Prince Wilhelm Regiment (112th Infantry) in 1912. Following a severe bout of rheumatism resulting from months of exposure in the dampness of trench warfare, in 1916 he got himself transferred – through his connections with the Royal Family – to the *Feldflieger Abteilung* 25 ('Field Flying Unit' or FFA 25), initially as the observer for his friend *Leutnant* (Lieutenant) Bruno Loerzer, flying reconnaissance missions for the Crown Prince's Fifth Army. Drawn to the glory of being a fighter pilot, he completed flight training and eventually was posted to *Jagdstaffel* 26 ('fighter squadron', commonly shortened to 'Jasta'), commanded by Loerzer, in February 1917. During the next year he became a successful fighter pilot, and was made commander of Jasta 27, amassing 22 accredited victories.

Adroit at leveraging connections, Göring was an inscrutable and sometimes ruthless political animal; when 'Baron von Richthofen' replacement Wilhelm Reinhard was killed in July 1918 while test flying the revolutionary experimental Dornier D.I all-metal monoplane, *Oberleutnant* (1st Lieutenant) Göring got himself appointed as the next – and last – commander of *Jagdgeschwader Nr. 1* ('Fighter Wing No. 1'), the exceedingly famous and immensely popular 'Richthofen Flying Circus'. Inheriting the famous *Rittmeister*'s *geschwaderstok* (literally 'wing stick', a knobby walking stick that served as the unit commander's baton), Göring was not appreciated by unit members, one commenting:

General der Flieger Albert Kesselring, with *Ritterkreuz*, in 1940. (Bundesarchiv Bild 183-R93434; photographer unknown)

Richthofen flew and fought for the Kaiser and his Fatherland, not for decorations, but from a sense of duty. Göring fought until his ambition was satisfied. He had the *Pour le Mérite* and was commander of the most famous unit in the *Fliegertruppe* ('flying troops') … then he led the *Geschwader* with the stick from the ground.

Marrying into money and nobility by wedding Swedish Countess Carin von Kantzow on 3 February 1922, after the war Göring did a bit of barnstorming before moving to Munich to study political science, where he soon met and became enthralled with Adolf Hitler, joining the NSDAP (*Nationalsozialistische Deutsche Arbeiterpartei* or 'National Socialist German Workers' Party', commonly called 'Nazis') the next year. Göring came into his own as a Nazi politician, being elected to the Reichstag (German parliament) in 1928 and had himself appointed Prussia's Minister of the Interior, the position from which he controlled the state police. When Hitler came to power, Germany's new *Kanzler* ('Chancellor') appointed him to the Cabinet as a minister 'without portfolio'.

Once Hitler made Göring Air Minister, he oversaw the development and expansion of the Luftwaffe, mostly as a basis for increasing his own power and influence. Prior to Hitler beginning World War II, he only exerted his command authority over personnel moves and aircraft production. Göring certainly was no air power expert: he had not flown an aircraft since 1922; had no knowledge of, or experience in, air campaigning; and left doctrine, technological development and combat operations to the professionals, at least until the wartime employment of '*his* air force' put his prestige at risk.

Göring's primary two subordinates during the *Luftschlacht um England* ('Air Battle for England') had vastly different backgrounds and personalities. The first was another Bavarian, **Albert Konrad Kesselring**, who came from a decidedly middle-class background and, at 19 years of age, joined the army as an aspirant officer candidate in July 1904. After attending the Munich Kriegsschule the next year, he rejoined his unit, Bayerische Fussartillerie-Regiment Nr. 2 ('2nd Bavarian Foot Artillery Regiment') and was commissioned as a *Leutnant* on 8 March 1906. Two years later he attended the 18-month Artillerie und Ingenieurschule ('Artillery and Engineer School') and in June 1912 trained as an artillery balloon observer. At the start of World War I he was the battalion commander's adjutant, proving so adept at handling administrative and operational matters that he moved steadily upwards and – after graduating from the Kriegsacademie as a general staff officer – he finished the war on the staff of the III. Königlichen Bayerischen Armee Korps ('Royal Bavarian Army Corps').

Following the war he commanded an artillery battery, then a battalion, before settling into the staff as a colonel in 1933. An able administrator and a capable commander, Kesselring impressed his superiors as an 'efficiency expert'; consequently, in October 1933, he was one of the talented officers transferred to the clandestine Reichsluftwaffe, becoming the chief of administration. At age 48 he learned to fly and, as Göring increased the power and prestige of the new Luftwaffe, he was promoted to *Generalleutnant* in April 1936. With Wever's death three months later, Göring selected him to be the chief of the *Luftkommandoamt* ('Air Force Command Bureau', essentially the Luftwaffe COS).

A stocky, balding man whose pleasant disposition exuded a cheerful confidence, Kesselring worked diligently to organize a new military service that seemed to be expanding out of control, but soon found himself embroiled in the 'power politics' of Göring's realm, especially when attempting to deal with his deputy, the ruthlessly ambitious Erhard Milch, who wanted the job for himself. The political intrigues of the job soon found him looking to return 'to the field' and after only nine months in office, Kesselring was promoted to *General der Flieger* and made commander of Luftkriegskommando III ('Regional Air Command 3') which later became Luftwaffengruppenkommando 1 and later Luftflotte 1 ('Air Fleet 1') in April 1939 and led that command in the conquest of Poland that September.

When Felmy was sacked following the embarrassing 'Mechelin Incident' – during which a courier aircraft mistakenly landed in Belgium with the Luftwaffe's paratrooper plans for *Fall Gelb* – Kesselring was given command of Luftflotte 2 and, once again, led his command effectively and with great distinction, this time in the conquest of Holland and Belgium, contributing to the ultimate success of Hitler's *Westfeldzug*.

While Kesselring exhibited a congenial demeanour and a quick, warm smile, the commander of Luftflotte 3 was well known for his abrasive personality. Born in 1885, **Hugo Otto Sperrle** was the son of a Württemberg brewer who, joining the army at age 18, became a *Leutnant* in the Infanterie-Regiment 'Großherzog Friedrich von Baden' Nr. 126. Also trained as a balloon observer, Sperrle easily transferred to the expanding Luftstreitkräfte ('Army Air Service') as aeroplanes took over more of that role, first as an observer with FFA 4, later commanding FFA 42. Becoming a pilot, he was badly injured in a crash in February 1916 and, after a long recovery, commanded an observer school before being appointed as *Kommandeur der Flieger* ('Aviation Commander') for 7. Armee covering Alsace at the southern end of the front.

Following the war he served in the *Freikorps* (right-wing paramilitary militia who fought against communist uprisings in post-World War I Germany) commanding a handful of small government mail/army courier units – flying wartime AEG J.II and LVG C.VI ground attack/observation aircraft mainly between Berlin and Weimar – operating as *Deutsche Luftreederei* ('German Air Shipping Company'). During the mid-1920s he commanded the observation school at the clandestine training centre at Lipetsk, USSR, before being appointed to Wilberg's TA (L) Operations Desk in 1927. An intimidatingly big 'bear of a man' who squinted penetratingly through a monocle, Sperrle was considered a 'capable rather than brilliant officer' whose lack of tact and charm got him 'promoted' within 18 months to command an infantry battalion. Returning from this 'purgatory', Sperrle now had the credentials of the Reichsluftwaffe's expert on providing the air power that the army needed. During the Nazis' rampant expansion spurred between 1933 and 1935, he was chosen to lead the new Luftwaffe's first tactical command, Fliegerdivision 1 ('Flying Division'), which was established at Berlin in April 1934.

Two and a half years later, when Hitler decided to support Generalissimo Franco's Nationalist rebellion in Spain with air power, Sperrle was picked as the first commander of the Condor Legion, an independent, mobile, self-sustaining air force of 120 aeroplanes, 5,000 men, 1,500 vehicles, five flak (AA) batteries, and a nine-carriage 'barracks train'. Sperrle's command consisted of bomber and fighter groups of four squadrons each, supported by one reconnaissance and a maritime patrol squadron, initially flying 'first generation' He 51s, Ju 52/3ms, and Heinkel observation aircraft and floatplanes. These quickly proved outclassed by the Soviet fighters and bombers supporting the Republican forces, so he quickly received early versions of the Luftwaffe's 'second generation' warplanes, including the Ju 87 'Stuka'.

Returning to Germany in October 1937, Sperrle was promoted to *General der Flieger* the next month and, six months later, was given command of Luftwaffengruppenkommando 3, which later became Luftflotte 3, based in Munich. During the next year his command participated in the *Anschluß* ('annexation') of Austria and the subjugation of Czechoslovakia with active air power demonstrations. Drawn down to only two bomber wings and eight fighter groups (579 aircraft total), his command remained in reserve – in the event of a genuine military reaction from France – during the conquest of Poland in September 1939. Immediately afterwards, however, Luftflotte 3 was bolstered to three *Fliegerkorps* ('Flying Corps', the expanded version of the *Fliegerdivision*) with seven bomber and seven fighter wings (588 bombers and 509 fighters) – plus one *Stukageschwader* ('Stuka wing' with 103 Ju 87s) – for Hitler's *Westfeldzug*. By July 1940, Sperrle – now promoted to *Generalfeldmarschall* – was, despite his brutish, ox-like appearance, coarse wit and gross table manners, the most experienced air campaigner in the Luftwaffe.

Generalfeldmarschall Hugo Sperrle, with Ritterkreuz, in 1940. (NARA)

LUFTWAFFE ORDER OF BATTLE, AUGUST 1940

Reichsmarschall des Grossdeutschen Reiches Herman Göring
(Note: numbers represent available/serviceable aircraft strength on 13 August 1940)

Aufklärungsgruppe/ObdL 47/28 Various Types

LUFTFLOTTE 2 HQ: BRUSSELS, BELGIUM
GENERALFELDMARSHALL ALBERT KESSELRING
2.(F)/Aufklärungsgruppe 122   10/8
Ju 88/He 111

4.(F)/Aufklärungsgruppe 122   10/8
Ju 88/He 111

I. Fliegerkorps HQ: Compiègne, France
Generaloberst Ulrich Grauert

KG 1	I. Gruppe	27/23 He 111H
	II. Gruppe	35/33 He 111H
	III. Gruppe	32/15 He 111H
KG 76	I. Gruppe	29/29 Do 17Z
	II. Gruppe	36/28 Ju 88A
	III. Gruppe	32/24 Do 17Z

5.(F)/Aufklärungsgruppe 122 9/7 Ju 88/He 111/Do 17

II. Fliegerkorps HQ: Ghent, Belgium
General der Flieger Bruno Loerzer

KG 2	I. Gruppe	43/27 Do 17Z
	II. Gruppe	42/35 Do 17Z
	III. Gruppe	34/32 Do 17Z
KG 3	I. Gruppe	43/31 Do 17Z
	II. Gruppe	35/32 Do 17Z
	III. Gruppe	30/25 Do 17Z
KG 53	I. Gruppe	28/27 He 111H
	II. Gruppe	33/15 He 111H
	III. Gruppe	33/24 He 111H
	II./StG 1	38/30 Ju 87B
	III./StG 2	39/31 Ju 87B
	IV.(St)/LG 1	36/28 Ju 87B

Erprobungsgruppe 210 (fighter-bomber trials unit)
36/30 Bf 109/Bf 110 *Jabos*[5]
1.(F)/Aufklärungsgruppe 122 (as of 5 September)
9/6 Ju 88/He 111

9. Fliegerdivision HQ: Amsterdam, Netherlands
Generalmajor Joachim Coeler

KG 4	I Gruppe	36/17 He 111H
	II Gruppe	31/25 He 111P
	III Gruppe	35/23 Ju 88A

Kampfgruppe 100 (night pathfinders)
41/19 He 111H-3

Kampfgruppe 126 (naval support) 34/8 He 111H

I./KG 40 (naval support) 9/3 FW 200C
Küstenfliegergruppe 106 (naval support) 30/23 He 115/Do 18

3.(F)/Aufklärungsgruppe 122 11/9 Ju 88/He 111

Jagdfliegerführer 2 HQ: Wissant, France
Generalmajor Kurt-Bertram von Döring

JG 3	I Gruppe	33/32 Bf 109E
	II Gruppe	32/25 Bf 109E
	III Gruppe	29/29 Bf 109E
JG 26	I Gruppe	42/38 Bf 109E
	II Gruppe	39/35 Bf 109E
	III Gruppe	40/38 Bf 109E
JG 51	I Gruppe	32/32 Bf 109E
	II Gruppe (I./JG 71)	33/33 Bf 109E
	III Gruppe (I./JG 20)	36/34 Bf 109E
JG 52	I Gruppe	42/34 Bf 109E
	II Gruppe	39/32 Bf 109E
	I.(J)/LG 2	36/33 Bf 109E
JG 54	I Gruppe (I./JG 70)	38/26 Bf 109E
	II Gruppe (I./JG 76)	36/32 Bf 109E
	III Gruppe (I./JG 21)	42/40 Bf 109E
ZG 26	I Gruppe	39/33 Bf 110C
	II Gruppe	37/32 Bf 110C
	III Gruppe	38/27 Bf 110C
ZG 76	II Gruppe	24/6 Bf 110C
	III Gruppe	14/11 Bf 110C

5   Jabo is the German abbreviation for Jagdbomber, or fighter-bomber.

LUFTFLOTTE 3 HQ: PARIS, FRANCE
GENERALFELDMARSHALL HUGO SPERRLE

1.(F)/Aufklärungsgruppe 123
12/8 Ju 88/He 111

3.(F)/Aufklärungsgruppe 123
11/8 Ju 88/He 111

IV. Fliegerkorps HQ: Dinard, France
General der Flieger Kurt Pflugbeil

LG 1	I Gruppe	35/24 Ju 88A
	II Gruppe	34/24 Ju 88A
	III Gruppe	34/23 Ju 88A
KG 27	I Gruppe	38/23 He 111P/H
	II Gruppe	34/21 He 111P/H
	III Gruppe	31/23 He 111P
StG 3	I Gruppe	29/16 Ju 87B

Kampfgruppe 806 (naval support) 33/22 Ju 88A

3.(F)/Aufklärungsgruppe 31 (army co-operation)
Bf 110/Do 17/Hs 126

V. Fliegerkorps HQ: Villacoublay, France
Generallieutnant Robert Ritter von Greim

KG 51	I Gruppe	31/22 Ju 88A
	II Gruppe	34/24 Ju 88A
	III Gruppe	35/25 Ju 88A
KG 54	I Gruppe	35/29 Ju 88A
	II Gruppe	31/23 Ju 88A
KG 55	I Gruppe	39/35 He 111P/H
	II Gruppe	38/28 He 111P
	III Gruppe	42/34 He 111P

4.(F)/Aufklärungsgruppe 14 (army co-operation)
12/10 Bf 110/Do 17

4.(F)/Aufklärungsgruppe 121 8/5 Do 17/Ju 88

VIII. Fliegerkorps HQ: Deauville, France
Generalmajor Wolfram Freiherr von Richthofen

StG 1	I Gruppe	39/27 Ju 87R
	III Gruppe	41/28 Ju 87B
StG 2	I Gruppe	39/32 Ju 87B
	II Gruppe	37/31 Ju 87R
StG 77	I Gruppe	36/33 Ju 87B
	II Gruppe	41/28 Ju 87R
	III Gruppe	38/37 Ju 87B

V.(Z)/LG 1 43/29 Bf 110C
2.(F)/Aufklärungsgruppe 123 9/8 Ju 88/Do 17

2.(F)/Aufklärungsgruppe 11 (army co-operation)
10/8 Bf 110/Do 17

Jagdfliegerführer 3 HQ: Cherbourg, France
Oberst Werner Junck

JG 2	I Gruppe	34/32 Bf 109E
	II Gruppe	39/31 Bf 109E
	III Gruppe	32/28 Bf 109E
JG 27	I Gruppe	37/32 Bf 109E
	II Gruppe	45/36 Bf 109E
	III Gruppe	39/32 Bf 109E
JG 53	I Gruppe	39/37 Bf 109E
	II Gruppe	44/40 Bf 109E
	III Gruppe	38/35 Bf 109E
ZG 2	I Gruppe	41/35 Bf 110C
	II Gruppe	45/37 Bf 110C

LUFTFLOTTE 5 HQ: STAVANGER, NORWAY
GENERALOBERST HANS-JÜRGEN STUMPFF

X. Fliegerkorps HQ: Stavanger, Norway
Generalleutnant Hans Geisler

KG 26	I Gruppe	30/29 He 111H
	III Gruppe	32/32 He 111H
KG 30	I Gruppe	40/34 Ju 88A
	III Gruppe	36/28 Ju 88A/C
JG 77	II Gruppe	39/35 Bf 109E
ZG 76	I Gruppe	34/32 Bf 110C/D

Küstenfliegergruppe 506 (naval support)
24/22 He 115

1.(F)/Aufklärungsgruppe 120
4/4 Ju 88/He 111

1.(F)/Aufklärungsgruppe 121
7/5 Ju 88/He 111

2. and 3.(F)/Aufklärungsgruppe 22
(army co-operation)12/6 Do 17M/P

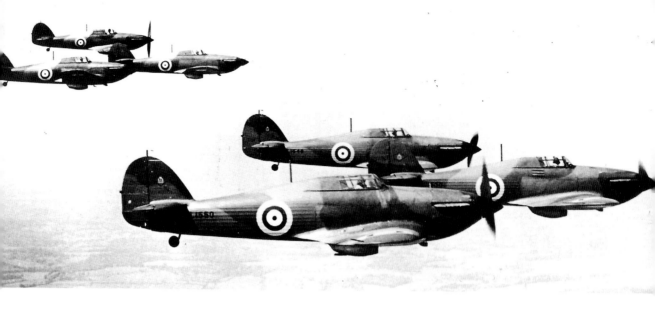

DEFENDER'S CAPABILITIES
Fighter Command

Doctrine: 'Intercept early and attrite heavily'

Fighter Command's pilots were hamstrung by its restrictive flying regulations, peacetime training, tight air-display formations, and scripted, choreographed tactics, flying in three-aeroplane 'vics' that limited firepower, manoeuvrability, and defensive lookout. (Private Collection)

In June 1940, when the panzers arrived at the French shores of the English Channel, the Luftwaffe faced the most sophisticated and effective air defence network in the world. The genesis of this, history's first-ever integrated air defence system (IADS), was in the British awakening to the dangers posed by Hitler's bellicose regime, punctuated by his March 1935 unveiling of Germany's already-powerful and rapidly expanding Luftwaffe. Largely in response to this mounting menace, on 1 May 1936 the Air Ministry ordered the RAF to segregate the various, diverse elements of its 'Metropolitan Air Force' into mission-specific commands. One of the four results was Fighter Command, which took over RAF (nine biplane fighter squadrons and their stations), Territorial Army (AA artillery), Royal Engineers (searchlights), and Observer Corps elements of an organization called Air Defence of Great Britain (ADGB).

With memory of the indiscriminate night bombing by German naval Zeppelins and *Luftstreitkräfte* Gotha bombers still fairly fresh and air power theorists predicting much worse, ADGB was established in January 1925, with its primary organizational basis being the World War I observer network that tracked these German raiders through the night skies of England. Originally created by the Admiralty using police and the civil telephone/ telegraph network, the War Office assumed control in 1916 and placed it under the command of Major General E. B. Ashmore, who developed it into a reliable and responsive system using volunteer 'special constables' and a dedicated telephone network that reported – along with searchlight and AA units – to an Operations Centre at his HQ.

Ashmore's system was shelved after World War I but was resurrected only six years later when the Committee for Imperial Defence recognized the need for an air defence (AD) alerting network. Ashmore – now retired – was again put in charge and through a series of exercises was soon able to demonstrate 'excellent tracking … by day and night.' Observer posts were connected by direct telephone line to a reporting centre, which relayed cogent information to the ADGB HQ. By December 1925 the revitalized system covered Kent, Sussex, Hampshire and the eastern counties with 100 posts answering to four group HQs.

At the working level Ashmore introduced gridded operations room tables where 'plotters' used coloured 'counters' to track aircraft formations as they flew across the AD Zones. At each reporting centre, a 'teller' looked down from a balcony or elevated box to report the 'raid's' progress to ADGB HQ every five minutes, permitting the timely scrambling of – and interception by – the responding fighters. In January 1929 the system was passed to the RAF where it remained stagnant – except for the addition of a fifth group – until 1935–36 when it was doubled in size and organization, expanding into the north and west of England and to Scotland.

The limitation of the system – in addition to requiring daylight and clear skies – was that approaching bombers had to virtually 'make landfall' before the Observer Corps could begin visually tracking them. Even before Fighter Command was created, ADGB leadership recognized as fundamental the need for advanced (called 'early warning' or EW) knowledge of approaching bomber formations. The command's doctrine – such as it was in that day – was to intercept incoming raids as far out as possible and inflict maximum attrition on them, thereby reducing the amount of bombs dropped on targets.

The RAF's 'secret weapon': AMES Type 1 radar. Transmitting on 22.7–29.7MHz frequency, the crude technology used 350ft-tall steel towers to suspend the wire transmission aerials (seen to the right of the near tower) and broadcast on a 100-degree swath centred on a cardinal direction. (IWM CH 15337)

OPPOSITE RAF INTEGRATED AIR DEFENCE SYSTEM, WITH UNITS ASSIGNED, AS OF 12 AUGUST 1940

The AMES Type 2 Chain Home Low radar, developed by the RN to detect ships offshore, was much more advanced than the Type 1, and was equipped with two rotating aerial arrays. Operating on 200MHz frequency, the transmitting antenna was mounted atop a 185ft steel tower, with the receiver on a 20ft high wooden gantry, located beside the Operations Block at lower right. (IWM CH 15183)

Early warning radar system

Worried that the limitations of the visual raid reporting system would render it inadequate, in November 1934 the Air Ministry Director of Scientific Research, Mr H. E. Wimperis, asked Mr Robert Watt (later Sir Robert Watson-Watt), the Superintendent of the National Physical Laboratory's Radio Research Station, if there were any emerging technologies that could be used to destroy approaching bombers. Specifically Watt was asked if the dreaded 'death ray' popularized by lurid science-fiction magazines had any real potential. Watt dismissed the 'death ray' idea, but added that radio waves – reflected off flying aeroplanes as 'electronic echoes' – could potentially provide early detection of approaching aircraft. He elaborated his theories in his February 1935 report 'Detection and Location of Aircraft by Radio Methods' and Wimperis arranged a meeting between himself, Watt, and the Ministry's scientific committee Air Member for Research and Development, Air Vice-Marshal (AVM) Hugh Dowding. The meeting proved both promising and prescient and, shortly thereafter, a test performed using a Handley Page Heyford biplane bomber and the BBC shortwave overseas transmitter at Daventry, Northamptonshire, conclusively proved the concept had merit.

Following the successful test, the Air Ministry authorized £10,000 for the development of Watt's primitive 'electronic echo' technology and after successful trials at Orfordness on the Suffolk coast, the first operational installation was built as the Bawdsey Research Station, located just south of the original site. The first lattice-work masts, used for suspending wire aerial arrays, were completed – and trials resumed – in March 1936, with the station soon reporting the detection of individual aircraft as far out as 62 miles (100km).

Watt's 'invention' was an essentially wide-swath (100-degree), range-only radar that was eventually designated the Air Ministry Experimental Station (AMES) Type 1. It was commonly called 'Radio Direction Finding' (RDF) to disguise the fact that it could not determine a target's bearing from the station (called 'azimuth'). Operating on 22.7–29.7MHz frequency with initial power output increasing from 450 to 750kW, two additional installations were constructed at Dover and Canewdon and, by August 1937, the three were connected to a 'filter room' where information was merged, redundancies eliminated, and triangulation (by intersecting range arcs) determined the target's location. (The sites attempted to use primitive radiogoniometer technology, first invented by Bellini-Tosi in

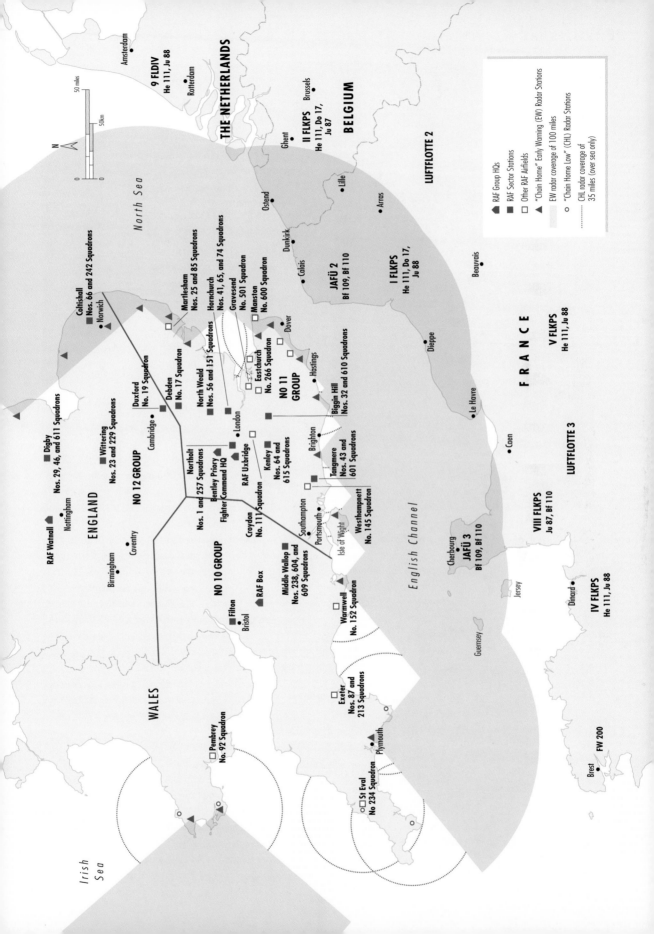

The bomb-proof underground Operations Room at Fighter Command HQ, Bentley Priory. Using the radar 'plots' provided by the adjacent 'Filter Room', Women's Auxiliary Air Force (WAAF) 'plotters' positioned markers indicating the incoming raiders' locations. From the balcony, officers made decisions on alerting Group HQs and sounding public air-raid alarms. (IWM C 1870)

1907, to determine target azimuth, but it proved almost completely useless in all but the most favourable circumstances.) Following another successful air exercise that month – during which formations of six or more aircraft were detected at 100 miles range – an array of 20 radar stations, called 'Chain Home' (CH), was authorized by the Air Ministry.

Meanwhile, the Admiralty had developed its own radar system for coastal defence against surface warships and low flying aircraft. Although lower powered (150kW) and shorter ranged, Mr C. S. Wright's 200MHz system was more advanced and, using a narrow (20-degree wide) beam that rotated 360 degrees, could more accurately determine a target's azimuth. The Air Ministry quickly adopted this – designated the AMES Type 2 'Chain Home Low' (CHL) system – as a 'gap filler' to ensure a more comprehensive EW network – 30 stations supplementing the CH radar sites, all constructed by July 1940. These were backed up with the acquisition of two dozen smaller M.B.2 (mobile base) sets that could be erected to replace destroyed or damaged permanent units.

The CHL sites provided their information by telephone to the nearest CH station which were all tied by 'land lines' to 'plotters' in Fighter Command HQ's 'Operations Room' where the progress of incoming aircraft was tracked. There the data was 'filtered' and the resulting 'raid information' was passed to Group HQ and its Sector Stations which vectored the defending fighters by radio to intercept them. Patterned after – and tying into – the Observer Corps network, which by this time numbered 30,000 personnel manning 1,000 observer posts and 32 reporting centres, and including the army's AA Command gun batteries and searchlights, this complex arrangement was exercised repeatedly and frequently to become as effective as its primitive technologies allowed.

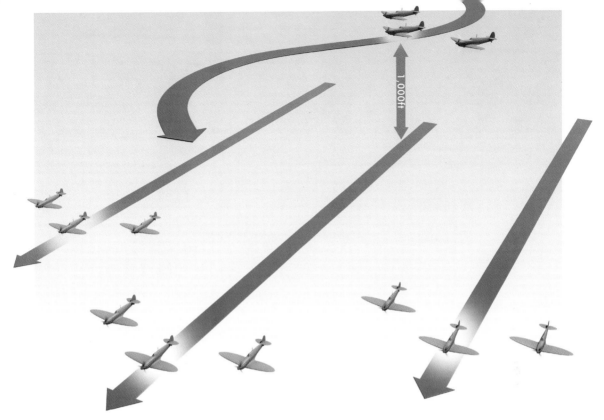

ABOVE RAF FIGHTER FORMATIONS

Typically an RAF fighter squadron of August–September was composed of 18 (sometimes 24) aeroplanes (including two in reserve) and 22 pilots, with the requirement to have 12 serviceable each day for combat operations. By August 1940 – learning from the savage lessons of the French campaign and the early clashes with Bf 109Es over the Channel – instead of the abhorrently rigid 'Fighting Area Attacks' formations prescribed in the 1938 RAF *Manual of Air Tactics*, each squadron generally flew as three three-aeroplane sections arranged in a V-shaped 'vic', with the 'vics' arranged in a 'V of Vs' formation. The fourth section flew behind – and stacked 1,000ft above – the main formation, weaving from side to side to discourage surprise attacks from astern.

Cruising at reduced speeds so that the 'weavers' could fly the longer serpentine flight path required to keep station on the main formation, the whole formation was at a tactical disadvantage when being attacked by Bf 109s using high speed 'slashing' attacks, and the 'weavers' were at a particular disadvantage in constantly offering their vulnerable 'six o'clock' to first one side then the other. High losses amongst the 'weavers' resulted in this practice being discontinued.

RAF fighters: capabilities, roles, and missions

When it was formed, the most advanced aeroplane in Fighter Command was the Gloster Gladiator – a fixed-gear, fabric-covered biplane with an enclosed canopy or hood – which was still in development. The first unit – No. 72 Squadron – became operational on type in February 1937, six months *after* the public debut of the fast, 'über-modern' Messerschmitt Bf 109 V1 all-metal monoplane fighter at the 1936 Berlin Olympics.

But the Luftwaffe was not the only organization developing high performance monoplanes. The days' rapidly advancing aviation technologies – spurred by the increasing payload, speed and range demands of the growing commercial airline industry – had finally produced bombers that were faster than opposing fighters, making them virtually immune to interception. To meet the threat posed by modern bombers, three things were needed: speed, heavy armament, and the ability to locate and close with approaching bombers.

To replace Fighter Command's slow, lightly-armed biplanes, in November 1934 the Air Ministry issued Specification F.5/34 for an 'interceptor monoplane' able to catch

The RAF's first modern fighter was the Hawker Hurricane Mk I. A relatively heavy, mixed-construction monoplane, the Hurricane was inferior to the Bf 109E in performance and manoeuvrability. (Private Collection)

the fastest bomber and bring it down with a two-second burst of machine gun fire. The Air Ministry required the advanced design – incorporating an enclosed cockpit and retractable undercarriage – to be capable of 275mph at 15,000ft altitude, be able to climb to 20,000ft in seven and a half minutes, and have a ceiling of 33,000ft. Based on recent studies, the design was required to mount a battery of eight .303in Browning machine guns that, firing at 1,150 rounds per minute, would in a two-second burst riddle the target with more than 300 bullet holes.

The first result was the Hawker Hurricane, a private venture designed by Sir Sydney Camm. A robust, stable, retractable-gear monoplane, the Hurricane was built using outdated mixed construction methods, which made it relatively heavy but permitted high production rates for the expanding Fighter Command. The prototype's maiden flight was on 6 November 1935 and it was judged to possess 'remarkable manoeuvrability and docility'. Powered by the new 1,030hp Rolls-Royce Merlin II V-12 liquid-cooled engine, the new fighter had a maximum speed of 320/325mph (depending on propeller type) at 18,500ft, a ceiling of 34,000ft and a range of 600 miles. The type became operational with No. 111 Squadron at Northolt in December 1937. Production 'ramped up' as the feared conflict neared, with 400 Hurricane Mk. Is being produced – equipping 18 squadrons – by the time Hitler started World War II. Ten months later Fighter Command had 32 Hurricane squadrons on its order of battle.

Augmenting the earlier, more numerous Hurricanes was the superb Supermarine Spitfire Mk I. Its performance and manoeuvrability virtually matched the Luftwaffe's Bf 109E. (IWM CH 27)

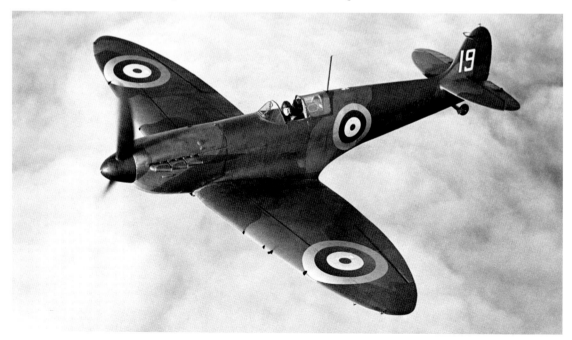

The second design to fulfil the 'interceptor monoplane' requirement was another private venture – Sir Reginald Mitchell's adaptation of his Schneider Trophy-winning high-speed design concepts – that resulted in the sleek, all-metal Vickers Supermarine Spitfire. An elegant design featuring a graceful and efficient elliptical wing planform – also powered by the Merlin II/III – its newer, more complex stressed-skin all-metal monocoque structure required skilled labour, greater effort and 2.5 times longer to construct than the Hurricane. The result was a sleek, fast interceptor capable of 355mph at 19,000ft – slightly faster than the Bf 109E – and a ceiling of 34,000ft. The Spitfire prototype followed its rather pedestrian stablemate into the air – and into its squadron service, with No. 19 Squadron at Duxford – only six months later, but its slower, more time-consuming construction process limited production rate. At the outbreak of World War II, Fighter Command fielded nine squadrons and added ten more in the next ten months.

The RAF's third single-engine 'day fighter', the Boulton Paul Defiant, was the result of a sadly misguided concept that totally ignored the realities of actual combat conditions. Mounting a powered, four-gun turret behind the cockpit – but with no forward firing weapons – the Defiant was intended to be flown alongside opposing bombers and 'exchange broadsides' as if it were a 'flying frigate' engaging enemy 'ships of the line', as in Lord Nelson's day. Heavy, relatively slow, and manoeuvring sluggishly, it had already proven easy prey for Messerschmitts – on 13 May, 264 Squadron lost five out of six in rapid succession when attempting to attack escorted Stukas (12.(St)/LG 1) over Moerdijk, Holland. Sadly, this disaster was masked by the glory of wildly exaggerated 'kill claims' – during 10–31 May Defiant gunners claimed 65 Luftwaffe aircraft shot down; German records reveal only 12 per cent of this total were actually lost. Even on the one occasion that the Defiant was able to use its intended tactic – 'trading broadsides' with Heinkel bombers (II./KG 27) over Dunkirk on 31 May – three were lost and only two bombers were shot down, with two more damaged. During the ensuing campaign, the Defiant, which equipped two RAF squadrons at the time, would get two more chances – both with tragic results.

Modified from the obsolescent Bristol Blenheim light bomber, the Mark IF (F for 'fighter') twin-engine, long-range 'fighter' was the RAF's answer to the Bf 110 *Zerstörer*. Unfortunately, while it had all of its counterpart's deficiencies and liabilities, it possessed none of its more favourable attributes. In May 1940, six Fighter Command squadrons were

The Boulton Paul Defiant carried a 1,500lb power turret on its back plus a gunner to operate it, giving the 'turret fighter' inadequate speed and sluggish manoeuvrability, making it extremely vulnerable to enemy fighter attacks. (Private Collection)

OPPOSITE RAF IADS: HOW IT WORKED

Fighter Command's radar, command and control, and interceptor/AA artillery interface system was history's first IADS. Incoming raids were detected by long range Chain Home EW radars, their locations and tracks being determined by intersecting range arcs from neighbouring CH radar stations and passed to FC HQ Filter Room. FC HQ was responsible for notifying Group HQs, sounding air raid alarms, and shutting down BBC transmitters to eliminate them as possible navigational aids for the attackers. Group HQ assigned each incoming raid to a Sector Controller for interception and alerted the appropriate AA batteries. Sector Controllers scrambled interceptors and, using radio, vectored them to engage the incoming raid.

Attempting to create a long-range 'fighter' from the obsolescent Bristol Blenheim light bomber, the Mark IF quickly proved completely inadequate and was soon relegated to becoming a radar-equipped night fighter. (Private Collection)

equipped with the type and learned the hard way that it was no fighter. On the very first day of Hitler's *Westfeldzug*, 600 Squadron attempted to interfere with the Luftwaffe's airborne assault on Rotterdam's Waalhaven airfield. Tragically, five out of six Blenheim IFs were shot out of the sky by Bf 110s (I./ZG 1) with the loss of six crewmen killed and two captured.

By this time the need for a radar-equipped 'night fighter' had become fully realized and in developmental programmes that rivalled the advance of the RAF's ground-based radar system, by 26 July some 70 Blenheim IFs were modified with the rudimentary Air Interception (AI) Mk III radar. Considered 'partially reliable', the AI Mk III had a maximum range of 3–4 miles down to a 800–1,500ft minimum range, which was beyond the reach of the aircraft's four .303 Brownings. The Blenheim's speed, which barely matched that of German bombers, was also patently inadequate. So it was with great hopes that the first Bristol Beaufighter Mk IF, with the improved AI Mk VI, was received for testing by the Fighter Interception Unit (FIU) at Tangmere on 12 August.

Finally, the third component needed to effectively engage and defeat Luftwaffe air attacks over England was these fighters' ability to locate and close with enemy bombers. While the coastal EW radar network could detect the incoming raids and the observers could track them overland (on clear days), getting the interceptors into a position to disrupt the raid with their eight-gun batteries would be the actual key to success. ADGB exercises in 1935–36 quickly proved the futility of allowing fighter formation leaders to 'dead reckon' – individually estimate an intercept heading and duration time to fly to it – a (usually inaccurately) predicted intercept point. Once an effective means of locating the fighters was developed – using a comprehensive high frequency direction finding (HF/DF) network – then the

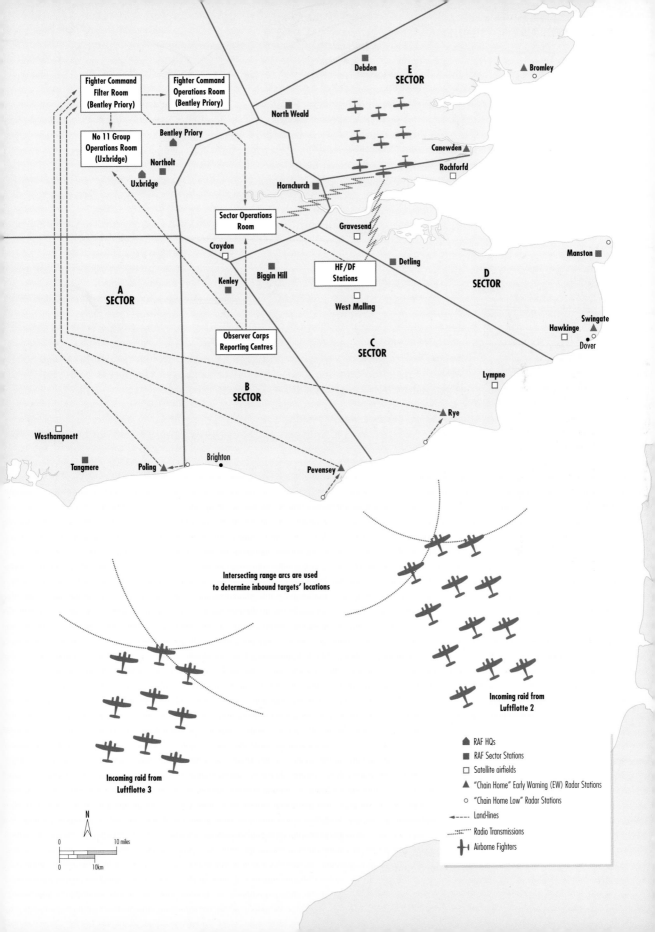

Fighter Command
Filter Room
(Bentley Priory)

Fighter Command
Operations Room
(Bentley Priory)

No 11 Group
Operations Room
(Uxbridge)

Bentley Priory

Northolt

Uxbridge

Debden

E
SECTOR

Bromley

North Weald

Canewden

Rochforfd

Hornchurch

Sector Operations
Room

Gravesend

Manston

Croydon

Detling

D
SECTOR

HF/DF
Stations

Kenley

Biggin Hill

West Malling

Hawkinge

Swingate

Dover

Observer Corps
Reporting Centres

C
SECTOR

A
SECTOR

Lympne

B
SECTOR

Rye

Westhampnett

Brighton

Pevensey

Tangmere

Poling

Intersecting range arcs are used
to determine inbound targets' locations

Incoming raid from
Luftflotte 2

Incoming raid from
Luftflotte 3

N

0   10 miles

0   10km

◆   RAF HQs

■   RAF Sector Stations

□   Satellite airfields

▲   "Chain Home" Early Warning (EW) Radar Stations

○   Chain Home Low Radar Stations

- - -   Land-lines

······   Radio Transmissions

✛   Airborne Fighters

calculations could be done in the Sector Station operations room (Ops Room) and vectors (intercept headings) would be radioed to the flight leaders. The interceptors were fitted with an automatic radio transmitter that broadcast – for 14 seconds each minute – continuously, called a 'Pip-Squeak', allowing each sector's HF/DF network to maintain accurate positions of up to four squadrons of interceptors, which were 'plotted' on the gridded map table in the Ops Room. Noting the position of the interceptors and the location of the raid, and its vector (direction, speed, and altitude), the Sector Controller calculated a 'cut-off' heading based on an imaginary isosceles triangle in which the line connecting the fighters and their targets and one formed by the bombers' flight path vector made up two of the sides. Because fighters were half again faster than their targets (roughly 300mph vs 200mph), the interceptors would usually arrive at the predicted intercept point early and orbit, allowing the fighter pilots to scan the skies to visually locate the approaching bombers. During 100 practice intercepts in late 1936, using this technique 93 were successful. Over the next four years the system was perfected through constant practice and exercises, resulting in a highly competent IADS that would be ready when it was most needed.

Commanders

Air Chief Marshal Hugh
C. T. Dowding
(IWM D 1417)

Responsible for the air defence of Great Britain was 58-year-old Air Chief Marshal **Sir Hugh Caswall Tremenheere Dowding**. Son of a Scottish schoolmaster, Dowding was educated at Winchester College and the Royal Military Academy before being posted to the Royal Garrison Artillery (RGA), serving in Gibraltar, Ceylon (now Sri Lanka), Hong Kong, India, and – finally – the Isle of Wight. New technologies intrigued him; in 1913, he attended the Vickers School of Flying, where he earned his aviator's certificate, and graduated from the army's Central Flying School the next year. Although returned to the RGA on the Isle of Wight, when World War I erupted he was immediately called to the Royal Flying Corps (RFC) as a reconnaissance pilot.

Initially posted to No. 7, then No. 6 Squadron, flying Farman MF.7s, MF.11s and HF.20s and Royal Aircraft Factory B.E.2s and B.E.8s, Dowding's senior rank quickly saw him posted as a staff officer to RFC HQ, which soon formed a detachment pioneering the use of radio for reconnaissance missions. His success in this rapidly developing field resulted in his posting to command the Wireless Experimental Establishment at Brooklands in March 1915, returning to the front to command No. 16 Squadron – primarily operating B.E.2cs – four months later. Although noted for being an 'efficient' leader, he was considered 'too reserved and aloof from his juniors' by squadron members – resulting in the nickname 'Stuffy'.

Nevertheless, Dowding's leadership potential was recognized and further advancement followed. After commanding Nos. 7 and 9 Wings, he was promoted to brigadier-general to command the Southern Training Brigade in the summer of 1917. Following the Armistice, he was rewarded with a permanent commission as a group captain in the RAF, commanding No. 16 Group and then No. 1 Group. Following service as chief staff officer at Inland Area HQ at Uxbridge and for RAF Iraq Command, in May 1926 he was appointed director of training at the Air Ministry and, after being promoted to AVM in 1929, he became Air Officer Commanding (AOC) Fighting Area, ADGB, and later joined the Air Council as Air Member for Supply and Research. By the time Fighter Command was formed on 14 July 1936 – and its HQ established at Bentley Priory, a large, old Gothic house near Stanmore on the northwest edge of London – the sum of Dowding's natural talents and military experience made him the single most qualified officer to lead it into the coming conflict.

Commanding the critical No. 11 Group, which defended London and south-eastern England, was 48-year old AVM **Keith Rodney Park**, a New Zealander who was educated at the Thames School of Mines and volunteered as an artilleryman at the outbreak of World War I. Winning a regular commission in 1915 after fighting with the NZ Expeditionary

Force at Gallipoli, he was posted to France where he was wounded so badly that he was relegated to Woolwich as an artillery instructor. By 1917 he had recovered sufficiently to volunteer for the RFC, rising to command No.48 Squadron flying the Bristol F.2B two-seat fighter, and was credited with five victories and 14 others 'out of control'.

Air Vice Marshal Keith Park (IWM CM 3513)

Following the war, Park was awarded a permanent commission and commanded the School of Technical Training and several RAF stations before appointment to Fighter Command as Senior Air Staff Officer (COS) in 1938. Tall, lean, and modest – and a 'tough but fair, inspirational leader' – Park was given command of No. 11 Group in April 1940, just in time for Fighter Command's response to the German invasion of the countries across the Channel from his seven sectors and to organize the RAF's air cover for the British Expeditionary Force's evacuation from Dunkirk. Facing Kesselring's Luftflotte 2, in August 1940 Park commanded 12 Hurricane, seven Spitfire and two Blenheim IF squadrons.

Facing Sperrle's Luftflotte 3 was No. 10 Group, established on 1 June 1940 and commanded by AVM Sir **Christopher Joseph Quintin Brand**, a 47-year-old South African who travelled to England and joined the RFC in 1915. Following flight training he served with No. 1 Squadron flying Nieuport 17 'scouts' and was credited with seven victories before being posted to England to help counter German Zeppelin/Gotha night bombing attacks. Commanding No.112 Squadron, flying modified Sopwith Camels from Throwley, Kent, he achieved his first 'night fighter' success, shooting down a Gotha bomber on 19 May 1918. With the *Luftstreitkräfte* discontinuing attacks on England shortly thereafter, Brand was transferred to command No.151 Squadron in France, where he was credited with four more nocturnal victories.

Between the wars Brand was posted to the Royal Aircraft Establishment (RAE), Farnborough, during 1925–27, serving as Senior/Principal Technical Officer. Two years later, he was sent to Abu Qir (Aboukir), Egypt, as Senior Engineering Officer, and later appointed Director-General of Aviation in Egypt from 1932 to 1936, returning to Britain to become the RAF's Director of Repair and Maintenance. Promoted to Air Commodore in 1938, he was arguably the most qualified air defence expert in the RAF. Brand's command consisted of only three sectors and eight squadrons, with most of Devon and Cornwall lacking coverage, guarded only by a flight of obsolete Gladiator biplanes based near Plymouth and two Hurricane squadrons deployed to Exeter.

Least qualified of FC's group commanders was AVM **Trafford Leigh-Mallory**, commanding No. 12 Group, protecting the Midlands with six sector stations and 14 squadrons. Son of a Cheshire cleric, the 48-year-old 'L-M' – as he was known in RAF circles – was educated at Magdalene College, Cambridge, and had applied to become a barrister in London when World War I broke out. He initially fought as a member of the South Lancashire Regiment and was wounded at Ypres. Recovering, he transferred to the RFC in July 1916 and, after flight training, flew B.E.2s with No. 7, then No. 5 Squadron before commanding No. 8 Squadron, which was heavily involved in army co-operation, directly supporting tank attacks in the Battle of Cambrai in 1917. Between the wars he pioneered air-ground co-operation, becoming the head of the RAF School of Army Co-operation before instructing at the Army Staff College, Camberley, and commanding No. 2 Flying Training School.

Air Vice Marshal Sir Quintin Brand (© National Portrait Gallery, London)

'Fussy, hotheaded and argumentative,' Leigh-Mallory was unscrupulously ambitious and acquired a reputation as an 'accomplished service politician and dagger man'. With conflict with Germany looming, he was appointed to command No. 12 Group in December 1937, being promoted to AVM in November the next year. Intensely jealous that Park – who was not promoted to AVM until July 1940 – was made commander of the premier, front-line No. 11 Group, L-M championed Squadron Leader (Sqn Ldr) Douglas Bader's 'big wing' concept – which ran counter to Fighter Command's doctrine of 'intercept early and attrite heavily' – as a means to discredit Park and eventually take his job.

RAF FIGHTER COMMAND ORDER OF BATTLE

ACM Sir Hugh Dowding HQ: Bentley Priory
(Note: numbers represent available/serviceable
aircraft strength at 1800hrs, 1 August 1940)

NO. 11 GROUP HQ: RAF UXBRIDGE
AVM KEITH PARK

Sector A   Sector Station: RAF Tangmere
Tangmere
43 Squadron	19/18 Hurricane
266 Squadron	18/13 Hurricane
601 Squadron	18/14 Hurricane
Fighter Interception Unit	7/4 Blenheim IF

Westhampnett
145 Squadron	6/9 Hurricane

Sector B   Sector Station: RAF Kenley
Kenley
64 Squadron	16/12 Spitfire
615 Squadron	16/14 Hurricane

Croydon
111 Squadron	12/10 Hurricane

Sector C   Sector Station: RAF Biggin Hill
Biggin Hill
32 Squadron	15/11 Hurricane
610 Squadron	15/12 Spitfire

Gravesend
501 Squadron	16/11 Hurricane

West Malling

Sector D   Sector Station: RAF Hornchurch
Hornchurch
41 Squadron	16/10 Spitfire
65 Squadron	16/11 Spitfire
74 Squadron	15/12 Spitfire

Manston
600 Squadron	15/9 Blenheim IF

Sector E   Sector Station: RAF North Weald
North Weald
56 Squadron	17/15 Hurricane
151 Squadron	18/13 Hurricane

Martlesham Heath
25 Squadron	14/7 Blenheim IF

Sector F   Sector Station: RAF Debden
Debden
17 Squadron	19/14 Hurricane
(deployed to Martlesham)	
85 Squadron	18/12 Hurricane

Sector Z   Sector Station: RAF Northolt
Northolt
1 Squadron	16/13 Hurricane
257 Squadron	15/10 Hurricane

NO. 10 GROUP   HQ: RAF BOX, WILTSHIRE
AVM SIR QUINTIN BRAND

Sector Y   Sector Station: RAF Middle Wallop
Middle Wallop
238 Squadron	15/12 Hurricane
609 Squadron	16/10 Spitfire
604 Squadron	16/11 Blenheim IF

Warmwell
152 Squadron	15/10 Spitfire

Sector W   Sector Station: RAF Filton
Filton (deployed to Exeter)
87 Squadron	18/13 Hurricane
(deployed to Exeter)	
213 Squadron	17/12 Hurricane

Pembrey, Wales
92 Squadron	16/12 Spitfire

St Eval
234 Squadron	16/10 Spitfire

Roborough (Plymouth)
247 Squadron	12/10 Gladiator

NO 12 GROUP HQ: RAF WATNALL
AVM TRAFFORD LEIGH-MALLORY
Sector G Sector Station: RAF Duxford
Duxford (Fowlmere)
      19 Squadron   15/9 Spitfire

Sector J   Sector Station: RAF Coltishall
Coltishall
      66 Squadron   16/12 Spitfire
      242 Squadron   16/11 Hurricane

Sector K   Sector Station: RAF Wittering
Wittering
      229 Squadron   18/14 Hurricane
Colly Weston
      23 Squadron   14/9 Blenheim IF

Sector L   Sector Station: RAF Digby
Digby 46 Squadron   17/12 Hurricane
      611 Squadron   13/6 Spitfire
      29 Squadron   12/8 Blenheim IF

Sector M   Sector Station: RAF Kirton-in-Lindsey
Kirton-in-Lindsey
      222 Squadron   17/14 Spitfire
      264 Squadron   16/12 Defiant

NO. 13 GROUP HQ: RAF BLAKELAW
AVM RICHARD SAUL
Sector N Sector Station: RAF Church Fenton
Church Fenton
      73 Squadron   16/11 Hurricane
      249 Squadron   16/11 Hurricane
Leconfield
      616 Squadron   16/12 Spitfire

Sector Airfield: RAF Usworth
Usworth
      607 Squadron   16/12 Hurricane
Acklington
      72 Squadron   15/10 Spitfire
      79 Squadron   12/10 Spitfire
Catterick
      54 Squadron   14/11 Spitfire
      219 Squadron   15/10 Blenheim IF

Sector Airfield: RAF Turnhouse
Turnhouse
      253 Squadron   16/12 Hurricane
      603 Squadron   15/11 Spitfire
Drem
      602 Squadron   15/11 Spitfire
      605 Squadron   18/14 Hurricane
Prestwick
      141 Squadron   12/8 Defiant

Sector Airfield: RAF Wick
Wick
      3 Squadron   12/10 Hurricane
Sumburgh
      232 Squadron   10/6 Hurricane
Aldergrove (N Ireland)
      245 Squadron   10/8 Hurricane
Castletown
      504 Squadron   17/13 Hurricane
Dyce/Grangemouth
      263 Squadron (one flight)
                    6/4 Hurricane

CAMPAIGN OBJECTIVES

The aim of [Operation *Sealion*] will be to eliminate the English homeland as a base for the prosecution of the war against Germany and, if necessary, to occupy it completely.

Hitler's Directive No. 16, 'On preparations for a landing operation against England',
16 July 1940

While the Luftwaffe fought its OCA campaign to attain air superiority over southern England, the *Kriegsmarine* collected some 2,318 river barges and modified them into makeshift assault landing craft called *prahme*, or 'prams' ('baby strollers'). (Bundesarchiv Bild 101II-MN-1369-10A)

Despite its impressive might and proven prowess, one of the Luftwaffe's most serious deficiencies was its lack of a proper General Staff. An outgrowth and redesignation of Luftkommandoamt, the ObdL was more like Göring's personal command staff rather than a service's High Command – more like Hitler's OKW than the army OKH or naval OKM. Its nine departments (*Abteilungen*) were gathered into two groups: the Operations Staff, containing Operations, Training, and Intelligence, under the Chief of Operations Staff, Generalmajor Otto Hoffmann von Waldau, and the *Generalquartiermeister* (Quartermaster General), *Generalmajor* Hans-Georg von Seidel, who supervised the logistics functions. (Both men reported to Göring through his COS, Jeschonnek.)

None of the departments was responsible for detailed planning of combat operations. This function was accomplished by operational echelons – the Luftflotten and Fliegerkorps HQs – while ObdL assigned and transferred units, determined operational objectives and priorities, disseminated suggested target lists and intelligence, and issued Göring's directives to the subordinate commands. Under the umbrella of ObdL's overarching 'guidance', it was easy enough for the Luftflotten and Fliegerkorps to develop concise but effective attack plans when conducting tactical operations for, and with, the army. In all previous campaigns Luftwaffe command echelons were attached directly to their respective or equivalent army command level – Luftflotten worked with *Heeresgruppe* (Army Group) HQ and Fliegerkorps were assigned to support a specific *Armeeoberkommando* ('numbered army'). The army commands, implementing OKH's offensive plans, provided operational direction and priorities to their attached Luftwaffe echelon, which would, in turn, apportion missions, allocate forces, and assign targets, thus directing their subordinate *Kampf-* and *Stukageschwadern* to attack enemy forces, defences, and installations to meet the army's desired objectives.

For the Luftwaffe, planning an air campaign independent of the army was an entirely new and untried endeavour for which its doctrine provided no guidance or foundation. Therefore, when faced with the necessity of doing so, there was not even an established concept of operations (CONOPS) in place as a basis for planning such an extensive military undertaking. Consequently, planning *Adlerangriff* began with a sporadic series of high level conferences and correspondence soliciting ideas on how to orchestrate an independent air campaign against Britain, with von Waldau's Operations Staff subsequently attempting to synthesize the different suggestions into a cogent strategy. While the two Luftflotten's units deployed to their new bases, regrouped, and replenished – and began conducting daily over-Channel operations implementing Hitler's War Directives Nos. 9 and 13 – this iterative process began in earnest on 18 July when Göring convened a meeting of his ObdL staff to discuss the anticipated offensive operations. Various staff sections prepared and presented papers covering their respective areas of responsibility.

These included a suggested – and rather sketchy – strategic targeting plan that was a hasty revision of Schmid's 22 November 1939 'Proposal for the Conduct of Air Warfare against Britain' and his oft-quoted updated *Studie Blau* intelligence summary. Also discussed were: 1.) the need to continue *Kanalkampf* ('Channel Battle') in order to train aircrews – many of whom were replacements for the 1,092 killed in the French campaign – and 2.) to develop and practice close co-ordination between bombers and Bf 109 fighter units. Bomber escort having been primarily the responsibility of Bf 110 *Zerstörer* units, this type's inadequacy in this role meant that the 'frontal fighter' units had to learn to do so – and that required practice to become proficient in this new mission. Finally, the need to establish an effective air-sea rescue capability was agreed and ordered.

Three days later Göring met with his three western Luftflotten commanders – Kesselring, Sperrle, and Luftflotte 5's *Generaloberst* Hans-Jürgen Stumpff – to discuss ObdL's recommendations and to emphasize that their staffs' planning should concentrate on attacking RN warships and naval bases. The latter was dictated by Hitler's 'War Directive No. 16, On Preparations for a Landing Operation against England', issued on 16 July. However, the conferees' chief concern was the anticipated heavy losses of Stukas and bombers to RAF fighters, so the attainment of air superiority returned to the fore as the overriding priority. The generals departed with instructions to submit their staffs' – and their subordinate Fliegerkorps' – assessments and suggestions for initial operations as soon as possible.

Now called 'Commanders' Assessments', these concise appreciations of the aims, tasks, and CONOPS for each Fliegerkorps were developed and passed to Luftflotten HQs, which appended their own comments and recommendations to them before forwarding them to ObdL, which was to distil them into a coherent and consistent set of priorities, objectives and target groups that would be applicable to all involved commands. To facilitate this synthesis process, ObdL's 'forward element' (codenamed 'Robinson') – Jeschonnek, von Waldau's Operations Staff, the Director of Training, and part of Schmid's Intelligence Department – moved, in its armoured HQ train, along with Göring's lavishly appointed personal train (codenamed 'Asia'), to a secluded siding near Beauville, France, about 50 miles north of Paris.

In one of his last duties in Berlin, while Göring hosted his top-level planning conference at Carinhall, his elaborate and luxurious hunting lodge north-east of Berlin, Jeschonnek represented his boss at Hitler's first 'joint service conference' for planning the proposed cross-Channel invasion of England, to be called *Unternehmen Seelöwe* ('Operation *Sealion*').

OPPOSITE LUFTWAFFE DEPLOYMENT FOR '*EAGLE ATTACK*', 12 AUGUST 1940

Despite its might and prowess, the Luftwaffe lacked a proper command-level planning staff, the air campaign planning process devolving to Luftflotte and Fliegerkorps HQs where the effort was largely *ad hoc* and conducted over telephone and teletype landlines. (NARA)

This conference resulted from the unsettling revelation that the army's and navy's concepts for conducting an amphibious offensive against Britain were widely – and wildly – incongruent. Unaware of what the Kriegsmarine' sea-lift capabilities actually were, OKH envisaged 'a river crossing on a broad front' during which the first wave – some 260,000 men and 30,000 vehicles – would be landed along a 235-mile front from Ramsgate to Lyme Bay during the first three days of the invasion.

Raeder and his *Seekriegsleitung* ('Naval Warfare Command' or SKL, the operations branch of *Oberkommando der Kriegsmarine*, or OKM) objected, proposing instead a 'narrow front' approach across the Straits of Dover, relying on minefields to protect the flanks, 'big guns' mounted for coastal artillery support, and the Luftwaffe's guarantee of 'uncontested German air superiority' to prevent any RN or RAF interference. Even if the necessary 'lift' (river barges modified into amphibious assault craft) could be acquired, with only the heavy cruiser *Admiral Hipper*, two light cruisers, seven destroyers, and 22 U-boats operational, the Kriegsmarine could hardly expect to protect the crossing from being ravaged by the RN's Home Fleet, which assigned the battleship HMS *Revenge*, nine light cruisers and 39 destroyers to anti-invasion forces while the bulk of the Home Fleet (four capital ships, two carriers, four cruisers and 30 destroyers) awaited the appearance of German heavy units. This much more limited option meant it would take ten days to get the army's 'first wave' forces onto British soil.

To arrive at a compromise the 'joint conference' was convened, but it failed to result in an agreeable solution, so Hitler scheduled a second meeting on 29–31 July, hosted at his Berghof retreat (near Berchtesgaden in the Bavarian Alps), where he went to arbitrate a Romanian-Hungarian-Bulgarian territorial dispute and begin reviewing intelligence on the Soviet Union. During this meeting *Generaloberst* Walther von Brauchitsch, the army commander-in-chief, and Raeder compromised on a medium-width frontal assault tentatively scheduled for 21–26 September, the 'window of opportunity' dependent upon tides and lunar illumination. The OKH's and OKM's approaches were consolidated into an overall provisional CONOPS, issued on 1 August as OKW's Directive No. 17. Commonly and erroneously called an 'invasion plan', this instruction was never more than a compilation of preparatory requirements that each service had to fulfil to make an operations plan viable.

Because the Luftwaffe was not represented at the three-day conference, Hitler's directive provided detailed instructions to Göring's air force:

> In order to establish the necessary conditions for the final conquest of England… I therefore order the Luftwaffe to overpower the English air force with all the forces at its command, in the shortest possible time. The attacks are to be directed primarily against flying units, their ground installations, and their supply organisations, but also against the aircraft industry.

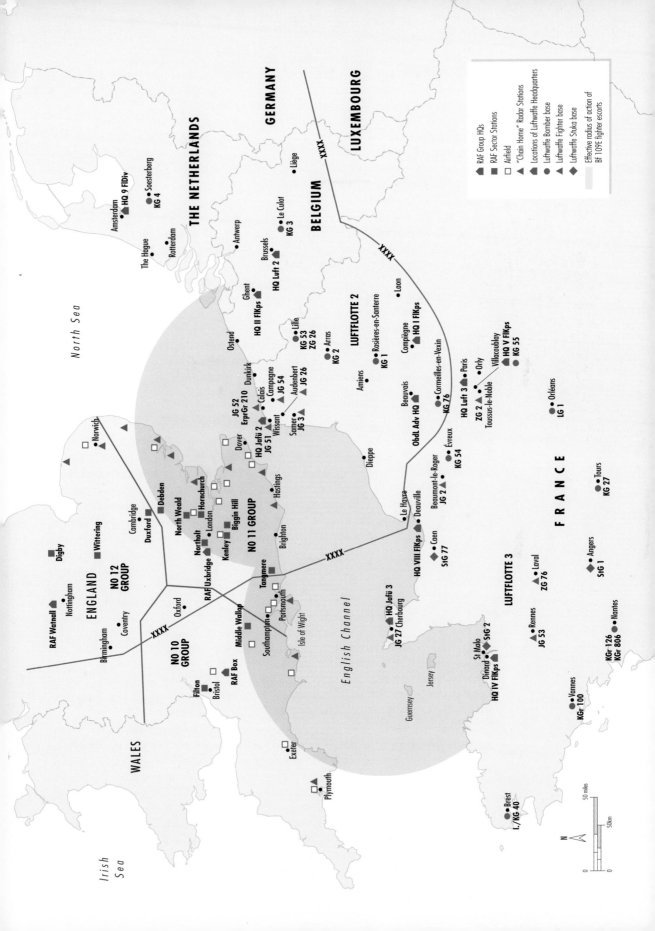

The Luftwaffe's primary mission was to mount an offensive counter-air (OCA) campaign to eliminate the RAF as a threat to any cross-Channel operation. Specifically, the Luftwaffe was directed that 'the English air force must be so reduced morally and physically that it is unable to deliver any significant attack against the German crossing.'

Following suit, the next day Göring's HQ – having reviewed the inputs from the Luftflotten and Fliegerkorps – issued its 'Preparations and Directives for "*Unternehmen Adler*" ("Operation Eagle")'. ObdL's 13-day *Adlerangriff* ('Eagle Attack') plan was designed to 'roll back' the RAF, bombing airfields and aviation industries in three phases, each advancing progressively – in 50km increments – closer to London. For daylight attacks London was considered the geographical extent of daylight bomber operations, dictated by the 125-mile operational range limitation of escorting Bf 109Es.

The objectives of 'Eagle Attack' were:

1. Neutralization of RAF Fighter Command forces – through aerial combat and bombing airfields – to attain air superiority over southern England,
2. Destruction of RAF forces – Bomber and Coastal Command units – that could interfere with a cross-Channel operation,
3. Destruction of RN units in ports and at sea along the England southern coast, but only if 'particularly favourable' targets presented themselves, and
4. Harassing (night) attacks against ports, communications, aircraft and aero-engine factories, RAF depots and bomber airfields.

To this directive was appended an expansive 'target list' taken primarily from Schmid's intelligence studies: RAF units and airfields of all kinds, factories producing aircraft, components and armaments. For the third objective, the appendix included RN ships and installations, and for the fourth, it contained a long list of ports and harbours that constituted 'blockade targets'.

For the two primary objectives Luftwaffe planners did not distinguish between fighter and other bases because, from their own experience, they were well aware that – given a bowser full of fuel, a busload of servicing personnel, a lorry full of ammunition and armourers, and a telephone line to HQ – a fighter squadron could operate from any suitable airfield. So all of the airfields along the southern coast and in southeast England would have to be rendered inoperative, and these were prioritized – not on a command-association basis but on a geographical basis – under the 'roll back' concept mentioned above.

From the outset, ObdL staff realized its knowledge of RAF installations in southern England was insufficient and had ordered a systematic photo-reconnaissance effort beginning on 27 June. Penetrating airspace against a viable IADS quickly proved to be a shockingly costly operation. Intercepted by radio-directed fighters, during the next five weeks the Aufklärungsgruppen lost 27 poorly armed reconnaissance aircraft – and Kampfgeschwader (KG) units augmenting them lost another 23 – even when escorted by as much as a Jagdgruppen of fighters.

Over the Channel, however, Luftwaffe operations were much more successful. Initially, these were relatively low intensity missions as the units settled into their new airfields in Holland, Belgium, and northern France, organized their supply and signals arrangements, replenished aircraft losses and trained replacement aircrews. During the much more intense six-week *Westfeldzug*, the two Luftflotten had lost 438 of their 1,120 twin-engine bombers. By 20 July the front-line bomber force was back up to 1,131 aircraft, with another 129 in Norway. Although inaugurated on 2 July, *Kanalkampf* began in earnest on 19 July with attacks on Dover harbour. Almost daily, three Fliegerkorps attacked convoys carrying coal from Wales to London, as well as other ships in the Channel, sinking 25 small steamers totalling 50,528 grt and four destroyers, prompting the Admiralty to suspend merchant shipping through the Straits of Dover during daylight. *Kanalkampf* culminated in late July with repeated attacks against Dover harbour that finally caused the RN to withdraw its destroyer flotilla north of the Thames Estuary.

While the RAF's responses to coastal and Channel attacks were disturbingly prompt and surprisingly vigorous, the *Jagdwaffe*'s strong escorts minimized losses (66 bombers and 22 Stukas lost to RAF fighters), and their 'fighter sweeps' (called *frei Jagd* or 'free hunting') and close escort (called *Jagdschutz* or 'fighter protection') shot down 64 Spitfires and Hurricanes during July. In the initial clashes, Bf 109E proved slightly superior to both the Hurricane and Spitfire when engaged above 20,000ft, where its faster climb rate, higher combat ceiling, heavier armament, and better diving capabilities proved decisive. Flown by veteran, combat-experienced pilots using superior tactics, the 'Emil' established its marginal superiority during *Kanalkampf*, with 37 lost to the two RAF day fighter types, creating a roughly 1.7:1 victory-to-loss ratio (or 'kill ratio') that would prove remarkably consistent throughout the campaign. On 1 August 1940, the two Luftflotten possessed 702 serviceable Bf 109Es (of 813 total) in 24 *Jagdgruppen*. To oppose them, two days later Fighter Command mustered 570 Spitfires and Hurricanes (367 serviceable), along with another 138 unsuitable Blenheims and Defiants, and 1,434 pilots. To the 570 day fighters can be added the 264 newly-built Hurricanes and Spitfires at the depots awaiting unit assignment as of 11 August.

On 1 August, Göring held a large conference (*Besprechung*) at the Wehrmacht occupation HQ in The Hague to finalize the plan for opening the air attack on Britain. He had decided to begin 'Eagle Attack' with a feint attack on London, under cover of which the main blow would fall upon Fighter Command installations. The first wave would consist of a relatively small group of Stukas, bombers, and Bf 109s to draw enemy fighters into the air, followed 10–15 minutes later by a wave of massed fighters to heavily engage them. The main bomber formations, escorted by Bf 110s, would follow about an hour later to deliver heavy attacks on RAF airfields, intent on catching

For the five weeks before 'Eagle Attack' began, the Luftwaffe flew approximately 1,300 sorties against British shipping in the Channel, sinking 25 steamers totalling over 50,000 tons. (NARA)

the surviving Spitfires and Hurricanes on the ground, refuelling and rearming. The initial effort would be followed by two similar attacks in the afternoon, with Generallieutnant Robert Ritter von Greim's V. Fliegerkorps reserved for night bombing RAF bomber bases in eastern England. This pattern would be repeated on the next two days with attacks against airfields closer to London.

It took five days of conferences with fighter and bomber *Gruppenkommandeure* ('group commanders') and map exercises with pilots and aircrew to familiarize all involved with the plan of attack, and Göring hosted a final *Besprechung* at Carinhall on 6 August to ensure all preparations were complete. The opening attack – called *Adlertag* ('Eagle Day') – was set for next day, but the weather turned bad over England, forcing postponement for five days.

THE CAMPAIGN

From Reichsmarsall Göring to all units of Luftflotten 2, 3 and 5.
Subject: Operation Adler.
Within a short period you will wipe the English Air Force from the sky.
Heil Hitler

Hermann Göring, Communique to the commanders of
Luftflotte 2, 3, and 5, 8 August 1940

First strikes on Chain Home: 12 August

The Junkers Ju 88A *Schnellbomber* was the newest and best Luftwaffe bomber but was plagued with problems such as inflight fires, limiting its use. (NARA)

The Luftwaffe opened *Adlerangriff* with a series of attacks that established the pattern of air operations against viable IADS for decades to follow – up to and including the initiation of Operation *Desert Storm*. During the intervening 50-plus years it became axiomatic that the first step of a successful offensive air campaign was to 'blind' the defenders by destroying their radars. By noting the continuous electronic emissions emanating from the mysterious towers that dotted the English coastline and by listening to RAF voice frequencies during *Kanalkampf*, Martini's *Funkhorchdienst* ('radio monitoring service') determined that German aircraft were being detected by the coastline installations and RAF interceptors were being directed by radio from certain airfields using information somehow derived from their emissions. Martini insisted that the first attacks of *Adlerangriff* must knock out the *Funkstationen mit Sonderanlagen* ('radio stations with special installations') and on 3 August Jeschonnek directed Sperrle and Kesselring to plan their opening attacks accordingly.

The two Luftflotten commanders took decidedly different approaches to attacking the CH radar sites in their respective areas of responsibility (AORs). Against the four sites along the southeast coast, Kesselring decided to use the newly arrived Bf 109E-4/B and Bf 110C-6/D-0 fighter-bombers under evaluation by *Erprobungsgruppe* 210 ('Trials Group 210', abbreviated ErprGr 210). Originally established to evaluate the Stuka's intended replacement, the twin-engine Messerschmitt Me 210, that type's incurable developmental problems resulted in the unit being equipped instead with bomb-carrying versions of the Luftwaffe's standard single- and twin-engine fighter types to prove the fighter-bomber concept and develop equipment and tactics to make them more effective in the ground-attack role. Against the Ventnor RDF station on the Isle of Wight, Sperrle used a whole group of Ju 88s (II./KG 51) in the dive-bombing mode.

Mid-morning, following a fighter sweep of 'Emils' (II./JG 52) that engaged a dozen Spitfires (610 Sqn), *Hauptmann* Walter Rubensdörffer led 12 bomb-laden Bf 110s and eight Bf 109s northwards from Calais at 18,000ft, then – short of Dover – turned south-west to parallel the English coastline, peeling off his squadrons as they passed abeam their targets. Due to the lack of azimuth tracking capability and confusing range information by passing abeam the radar sites, FC Filter Room labelled the contact an 'X raid' ('doubtful origin, possibly friendly aircraft') and no interceptions were attempted. The Bf 109s dropped eight SC 250 (551lb) bombs on the Swingate (Dover) CH radar and the Bf 110s scattered eight SC 500 (1,102lb) bombs on the sites at Pevensey and Rye. The resulting damage was sufficient to knock each of them 'off the air', causing a 100-mile wide gap in the radar chain for three to six hours. The bomb blasts failed to topple the aerial masts and none of the vital transmitting/receiving blockhouses were hit, so operations resumed once repairs were made.

Much more effective was Sperrle's midday attack against the Ventnor radar. Initially steering almost directly for Brighton, Oberst Johann-Volkmar Fisser led 68 Ju 88As (KG 51 and III./KG 55) northwards, outflanking the electronic swath of the Ventnor station, then turned west, crossing in front of the Poling radar station and heading into the Solent. Behind Ventnor's coverage, Poling's lack of azimuth capability and the confusing approaching-then-receding range information baffled the 'track-tellers', resulting in heavy, unopposed attacks against Portsmouth's city centre, docks, and naval base, killing 96 people. (Portsmouth was the RN's primary base on the west end of the Channel and had to be neutralized for *Seelöwe* to proceed.) Meanwhile 15 others (II./KG 51) turned south from over the Solent and struck the Ventnor station from behind, dropping 15 of their 74 bombs into the complex. While again the aerial masts were not felled, damage was extensive, knocking the site 'off line' for three days. As the bombers began egressing the battered target, Brand's interceptors (152, 213 and 609 Sqns) finally arrived, pursuing the fleeing raiders at low level and shooting down nine – including Fisser's – before the escorts, circling high above, dived into the running fight.

While the No. 11 Group radars were off the air, Luftflotte 2 hit three coastal 'satellite airfields': Lympne, Hawkinge, and Manston. At 0930 Do 17Zs (I./KG 2) ploughed up Lympne's landing grounds with 140 small SC 50 (110lb) bombs, rendering it unusable for the day. Shortly afterwards Ju 88s (II./KG 76) destroyed Hawkinge's workshops and two hangars and cratered the landing grounds, knocking it out for 24 hours. Just after midday, ErprGr 210 attacked Manston, followed by 18 Dorniers (I./KG 2 again) that gutted workshops, wrecked two hangars, and cratered landing grounds with 150 bombs, the attack's ferocity driving the base's personnel into underground shelters from which many refused to emerge for days.

Adlertag (Eagle Day): 13 August

With a forecast of bad weather the next morning, Göring postponed *Adlertag*, which was intended to be an 'annihilating reprisal for English attacks on the Ruhr'. However, inevitably some units did not get the word. The most devastating morning raid was by *Oberst* Johannes

Fink's KG 2, which sent 74 Do 17Zs to bomb Eastchurch airfield and Sheerness naval base on the Isle of Sheppey in the Thames Estuary.

Descending beneath the clouds (and most of the radar coverage) the Luftwaffe's low-flying experts were spotted as they crossed the coast, but the adverse weather foiled effective Observer Corps tracking. Alerted late, Park scrambled five squadrons that climbed above the clouds, allowing 44 Dorniers to bomb Sheerness unopposed while 30 others (III./KG 2) struck Eastchurch in two waves. Dropping over 100 high explosive (HE) bombs from only 1,500ft altitude, the surprise attack wrecked the barracks, killing 16 and injuring 48, damaged every hangar, destroyed all 266 Squadron's ammunition and one Spitfire, as well as five Coastal Command (53 Sqn) Blenheim IV patrol bombers. Arriving late, pursuing 111 and 151 Squadrons shot down five Dorniers during egress.

The 'annihilating reprisal' was finally launched mid-afternoon with Sperrle sending a massive 40-mile-wide wave of 58 Ju 88s (I. and II./LG 1) to bomb Boscombe Down, Worthy Down, and Andover airfields and 52 Stukas (I./StG 1 and II./StG 2) against Warmwell and Yeovil, followed by Kesselring despatching Stuka raids against Rochester and Detling airfields. Alerted late by the new, small, short-ranged CH station at Worth Matravers, Brand and Park scrambled eight squadrons – 77 fighters. Weather prevented most of the planned airfield attacks, so I./LG 1 bombed Southampton instead. Late detection resulted in heavy damage and civilian casualties in Southampton's port and residential areas; the interceptors eventually engaged, shooting down six Junkers. The slower Stukas were soon devoid of fighter escort (II./JG 53) as the 'Emils' turned for home due to low fuel. Shortly afterwards 609 Squadron Spitfires engaged, shooting down six – the 21 survivors turned back and bombed Portland. Due to extensive cloud cover at 3,000ft, II./StG 2's 25 Stukas could not find Yeovil and, unengaged, they also bombed Portland.

Typical CH radar station. The masts supporting the wire transmitting aerials are to the left, arranged in a line orientated on a cardinal direction. The all-important receiving aerials were 'strung' from the four 240ft tall wooden towers, arranged in a square radiogoniometer pattern, to the right. (IWM CH 15173)

Coastal Observer post. When the EW radars became unserviceable, these were usually the initial sources of information – position, numbers, direction, and altitude – that there was a 'raid inbound'. (NARA)

Luftflotte 2's raids followed about an hour afterwards, but most of the attackers could not locate their targets, which were veiled in low clouds. In a strike intended to help enable *Seelöwe*, at 1716hrs IV.(St)/LG 1 struck Detling, hitting three mess halls and killing 78 people, including the station commander, destroying the operations block, and cratering the taxiways and hardstands, destroying 22 Coastal Command Avro Anson maritime reconnaissance aircraft (500 Sqn). The vulnerable Stukas suffered no loss because a well-timed *freie Jagd* sweep by JG 26 and ZG 26 effectively prevented interception.

Overall, the Luftwaffe had launched 1,484 sorties and losses were high – 42 aircraft, with 89 pilots and aircrew killed or captured. While 47 RAF aircraft were destroyed in the airfield attacks, only one was a fighter, to which can be added 13 lost in aerial combat, with three pilots killed and two more severely burned.

Following *Adlertag*'s anti-climactic disappointment, persistent cloudy skies continued to throttle Luftwaffe operations, with only 91 bomber and 398 fighter sorties flown the next day. ErprGr 210 successfully struck Manston, destroying four hangars and three Blenheim

Attacking the Chain Home radar sites

To 'open the door' for *Adlertag*'s large attacks scheduled for the next day, Luftflotten 2 and 3 attempted to knock out five Chain Home EW radar sites, four of them in the former's AOR, mostly along the Kent and Sussex coastlines. Kesselring assigned this mission to the newly-arrived Erprobungsgruppe 210 (ErprGr 210), an experimental *Jabos* (fighter-bomber) trials unit that had proven particularly effective dive-bombing ships in the Channel. While the *Gruppenkommandeur*, *Hauptmann* Walter Rubensdörffer, led his *stabschwarm* ('staff flight') against the inland CH station at Dunkirk, near Canterbury, 1. Staffel (Bf 110C-6s) hit Pevensey, 2. Staffel (Bf 110D-0s) struck Rye, and *Oberleutnant* Otto Hintze's 3. Staffel attacked the Swingate CH site near Dover with eight Bf 109E-4/Bs.

Following a confusing approach that turned to parallel the English coastline westbound, the four individual formations peeled off northwards to attack their assigned targets. This tactic placed Hintze's 3. Staffel behind the broadcast 'swath' of the Swingate CH radar and perpendicular to the Rye CH radar, resulting it being unseen by both. In order to avoid the balloon barrage and extensive AA batteries protecting Dover, Hintze led his formation across Langdon Bay, to the east of the port, where individual aircraft then peeled off to attack the four prominent 350ft-tall Chain Home aerial masts with SC 250 (250kg/551lb) general purpose bombs. After delivering his weapon, Hintze turned hard to the right to reform his *staffel* and watch for patrolling RAF fighters while his wingman dropped his own bomb. Third to attack was *Oblt* August Wiing, flying 'Yellow 3'.

Although the bombing by the eight *Jabos* was reasonably accurate, the bomb blasts failed to topple the steel lattice masts but damaged them slightly and destroyed several of the huts inside the compound. However, the transmitting and receiving blocks, and the relatively unprotected 'watch office', where the plotting of radar returns was conducted, were unharmed. Repairs restored the AMES Mk I radar to operation in the early afternoon.

IFs (600 Sqn), while KGs 27, 53, and 55 attacked eight airfields in small raids that did little damage. The attack on Middle Wallop hit the hangars and offices of 609 Squadron but lost the He 111 carrying KG 55 *Kommodore Oberst* Alois Stoeckl and Luftgau VIII COS *Oberst* Walter Frank, killing both. Additionally, various *freie Jagd* sweeps and Stuka attacks on Channel shipping resulted in further fighter combat. In the first three days of *Adlerangriff* Fighter Command lost 36 Spitfires and Hurricanes while the *Jagdwaffe* lost 26 'Emils'.

Adlerangriff Phase I (Eagle Attack Phase I): 15–18 August

Until further orders, operations are to be directed exclusively against the enemy air force, including targets of the enemy aircraft industry allocated to the different Luftflotten… Our night attacks… should, where possible, be directed against air force targets.

Hermann Göring, Carinhall Conference,
Address to ObdL Staff, paragraph 6, 15 August 1940

The bad weather that precluded most missions over England on 14 August was forecast to remain the following day, so Göring convened another commanders' meeting at Carinhall, this one to post-mortem the mistakes of *Adlertag*. Despite the departures of Kesselring, Sperrle, and the Fliegerkorps commanders, plans were in place to renew bombing operations following the *Adlertag* pattern, only this time with *Generaloberst* Hans-Jürgen Stumpff's Scandinavian-based Luftflotte 5 included. After three days of combat, Luftwaffe planners expected Dowding to reinforce Park and Brand's commands with units from the northern groups, leaving the Midlands open to unopposed attacks. This proved to be a costly supposition.

While Göring was rebuking his commanders for their units' poor performance in the *Adlertag* operations, surprisingly, the weather began clearing rapidly and, in the absence of his commander, II. Fliegerkorps COS, *Oberst* Paul Deichmann, ordered the planned attacks to be launched. II. Fliegerkorps' first wave – repeating attacks on Hawkinge, Lympne, and Manston – was intended to draw Fighter Command's attention away from Luftflotte 5's more northerly operations, so Stumpff's He 111s (KG 26) and Ju 88s (KG 30) were ordered to take off ('ordered off') as well.

The Aalborg- and Stavanger-based bombers took off around 1030hrs for their 450-mile/two-and-a-half hour flight to bomb RAF bomber bases at Linton-on-Ouse, Dishforth, and Driffield, home of No. 4 Group's six squadrons of Armstrong Whitworth Whitley twin-engine medium bombers. Once Stumpff's bombers were airborne, II. Fliegerkorps launched two *Stukagruppen*; these formed a wide line-abreast formation with a dozen Bf 110s flying on their right wing and three *Jagdgruppen* (II. and III./JG 26 and II./JG 51) sweeping ahead and flying top cover.

When the large, wide, ill-defined radar 'echo' was received by the Rye and Swingate CH stations at 1100hrs, the D-Sector controller established a two-squadron patrol inland from the coast, between Ashford and Dover, with three other squadrons patrolling along an interior line, while he waited for the broad radar return to resolve into individual raids. This indecision resulted in the 16 Stukas (IV.(St)/LG 1) arriving overhead Hawkinge unmolested – they tipped over into their dives as the British interceptors arrived. The crashing bombs demolished one hangar, damaged a barracks, and severed power cables to the Rye and Swingate radars, knocking them 'off-line' for most of the day. Some 26 Ju 87s (II./StG 1) pounded Lympne, the devastation preventing operations for the next two days, and the 12 *Zerstörers* viciously attacked Manston, destroying two Spitfires (54 Sqn) and causing 16 casualties.

Luftflotte 2's main effort for the day was a massive strike by *Oberst* Wolfgang von Chamier-Glisczinski's KG 3, 88 Do 17Zs taking off from their Belgian airfields at 1350–1406hrs. As they passed over the Pas de Calais they were detected as a large, broad radar return by the east coast CH stations, but as the escorting fighters – 130 Bf 109s from JGs 51, 52, and 54 – climbed into the electronic swath in front of the bombers, their larger, broader formation effectively screened the Dorniers, leading to a 'confused radar picture' in the Bentley Priory Filter Room. Another 60 Bf 109Es (II. and III./JG 26) crossed the coast at 21,000ft and high speed on either side of Dover on a large *freie Jagd* sweep and ErprGr 210 used the massive formation to mask its own flight northwards towards Harwich. Three airborne patrols – 24 Hurricanes and 12 Spitfires – were vectored against the approaching phalanx of raiders and four more squadrons were scrambled. The escorts proved almost impenetrable and the

During August and into September, frequently major strike missions had to be aborted because extensive cloud coverage blanketed the targets. (NARA)

Luftflotte 5 attempted to join in *Adlerangriff* on 15 August, sending 63 He 111s from Norwegian-based KG 26 to attack Bomber Command bases in northern England. (IWM HU 93724)

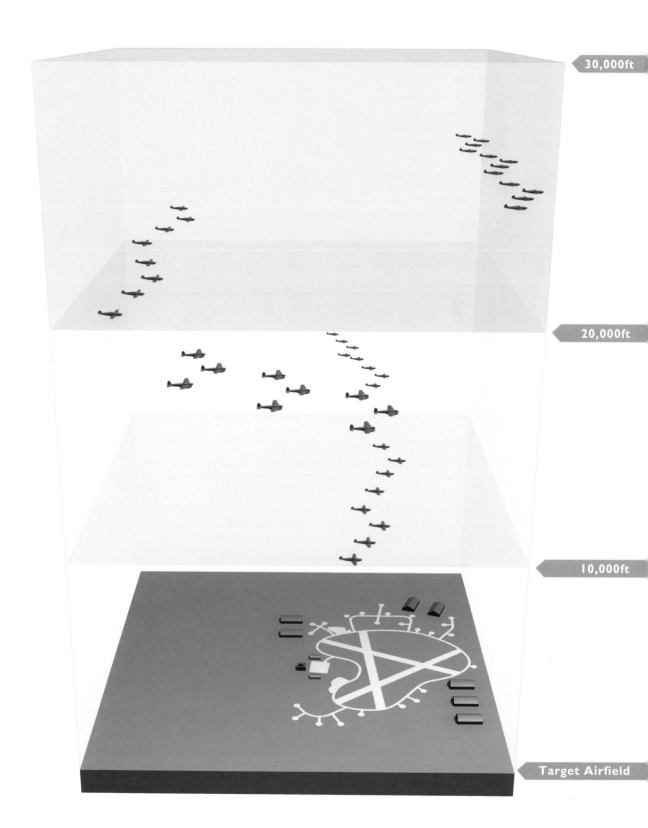

30,000ft

20,000ft

10,000ft

Target Airfield

OPPOSITE LUFTWAFFE MISSION COMPOSITION

Initially Luftwaffe doctrine called for each bomber wing (three *Kampfgruppen*, typically launching 18 bombers each) to be escorted by a *Jagdgeschwader*. In this case, one of the fighter wing's *Jagdgruppe* would range ahead of the combined bomber-fighter formation on a *freie Jagd* ('free hunt' or 'fighter sweep'), with the wing's other two *Jagdgruppen* positioned on the bomber formation's flanks, providing *Jagdschutz* ('fighter protection' or 'close escort').

The 'sweeping' *Jagdgruppe* would fly above 20,000ft altitude at the Bf 109E's normal engagement speed of 300mph and have complete freedom to engage any enemy interceptors that they spotted. The 'close escort' *Jagdgruppen* were 'tied' to the bombers, flying slightly above them and on their flanks, but having to 'keep pace' with the bombers, which flew at 190mph, and typically were not permitted to engage enemy interceptors unless they, or their charges, were threatened with attack.

Bf 110D with *Dackelbauch* ('Dachshund belly') non-jettisonable external fuel tank. These ungainly 1,050-litre (231 Imp gallon) tanks extended the type's operating radius beyond 800 miles, but at the expense of leaving the rear gunners behind and making the already poor manoeuvring *Zerstörer* more of a target than a fighter. (Private Collection)

Dorniers successfully attacked Rochester and Eastchurch, raining some 300 bombs upon the Short Brothers aircraft factory at the former.

Meanwhile, ErprGr 210's 16 Bf 110 and eight Bf 109 *Jabos* skirted the Kent coastline at low level and headed across the Thames Estuary towards Harwich, unseen by the east coast CH radars. The CHL radar at Walton-on-the-Naze detected them 18 miles off the coast – four minutes prior to landfall – and the *Jabos* swept in and attacked Martlesham Heath unopposed, wrecking two hangars, the station workshops, and No. 25 Squadron's equipment store. The devastated base was out of action for 48 hours. Nine Hurricanes (1 Sqn) from Northolt intercepted the egressing Bf 110s, but the Bf 109E-4s, having dropped their bombs, engaged and shot down three for no loss.

Luftflotte 3's attacks were concentrated against airfields within No. 10 Group's AOR. Launching at 1515–1530hrs were 27 Ju 88s (I. and II./LG 1), followed at 1600hrs by 47 Stukas (I./StG 1 and II./StG 2), to attack Andover, Worthy Down, and Warmwell. Heavily escorted by 120 Bf 109s (JGs 2, 27 and 53) and 50 Bf 110s (V.(Z)/LG 1, II./ZG 2, II. and III./ZG 76), the two formations were detected at 1700hrs by the degraded CH EW radars along the south-west coast. Brand scrambled two Hurricane squadrons (87 and 213 Sqns) from Exeter and 14 Spitfires (234 Sqn) from St Eval. The Spitfires engaged the escorting Bf 109s, but – outnumbered 4:1 – they were quickly overwhelmed. Facing spirited Hurricane attacks, the Stukas turned back, bombing Portland at 1730hrs. The faster Ju 88s forced their way through defending Hurricanes (43, 249, and 601 Sqns) and Spitfires (609 Sqn) to split, half bombing Middle Wallop, the others hitting Worthy Down and Odiham. Bombing from level flight at medium altitude, accuracy was generally lacking and losses were heavy, with five Ju 88s falling to Hurricanes.

The Bf 109E-4/B *Jabo* could carry two SC 50 (110lb) or a single SC 250 (551lb) bombs and make relatively accurate 45 degree dive-bombing deliveries. Once the bombs were released – or jettisoned if attacked – it reverted to its inherent fighter role. (Private Collection)

An hour later, Kesselring launched *staffel*-strength formations of He 111s (KG 1) and Do 17s (KG 2), escorted by four *Jagdgruppen*, to bomb Hawkinge and the radar stations at Dover, Rye, and Foreness, but little damage was done. Under the cover of these scattered raids, Rubensdörffer's ErprGr 210 approached London intending to attack the Kenley sector station from the north. Instead, his 15 Bf 110s and eight Bf 109s mistakenly struck London's Croydon airport – a 'satellite airfield' for 111 Squadron – hitting the terminal, hangars and nearby aircraft engine, radios, and parts manufacturers. No. 111 Squadron scrambled just before the raiders struck and intercepted immediately, shooting down six Bf 110s – including Rubensdörffer and his entire *Stabkette* ('staff flight').

Despite this sharp defeat, Luftflotten 2 and 3 enjoyed considerable success in the 1,950 sorties flown this day – the largest number during the entire Battle of Britain. Ten airfields had been struck, two of them knocked out for the next two days, and 28 British fighters were destroyed with the loss of 19 pilots captured, killed, or severely injured or burned. In addition to the seven *Jabos*, the two Luftflotten had lost 12 *Zerstörers*, 11 bombers and seven Stukas, and four Bf 109s over southern England, with the 'Emil' dominating 5.5:1 over the defending interceptors.

However, Luftflotte 5's disastrous midday raid against targets in northern England tipped the overall 'tally sheet' in the RAF's favour. From Stavanger came 63 He 111s (I. and III./KG 26), escorted by 21 Bf 110D-1/R1s (I./ZG 76). Approaching the Northumberland coast, *Oberst* Robert Fuchs' formations were detected by Anstruther CH radar in Fife at 1205hrs and, at No. 13 Group HQ, AVM Saul's fighter controller aggressively launched

One of the Luftwaffe's primary tactics was to attempt to attack RAF interceptors on the ground refuelling between sorties. Due to Fighter Command's effective air raid warning system this only occurred once, on 18 August, when a strafing attack by I./JG 52 caught 266 Squadron on the ground at Manston, destroying two fighters and severely damaging six more. (Tom Laemlein)

all available fighters to meet the incoming raid. Intercepted over the sea by 11 Spitfires (72 Sqn), the escorts immediately entered an *Abwehrkreis* ('defensive circle') and quickly lost seven shot down. Immediately afterwards, 18 Hurricanes (79 and 605 Sqns) attacked the Heinkels, scattering them – some bombed their secondary targets, Newcastle-upon-Tyne and Sunderland – and 13 more Spitfires (41 Sqn) intercepted them during egress. In all KG 26 lost eight He 111s; one Hurricane was so badly damaged by return fire, it crash-landed.

As the bombs were falling upon Sunderland, No. 12 Group's Staxton Wold CH radar reported a second raid inbound, apparently aimed at Church Fenton. This formation consisted of 27 Ju 88A bombers and 13 Ju 88C *Zerstörers* that formerly belonged to Z./KG 30, a dedicated 'heavy-fighter' squadron organic to the *Kampfgeschwader*. However, increasing size and effectiveness of Bomber Command raids on the Ruhr caused ObdL to order a number of *Zerstörer* units to be concentrated in the new *Nachtjagdgeschwader* (NJG or 'Night Fighter Wing') being established at Mönchen-Gladbach. Consequently, once the Norwegian campaign was successfully concluded on 8 June, the pilots and aircrews of Z./KG 30 were transferred to Germany to begin night-fighter training and transition to the Bf 110D, leaving their Ju 88Cs to be absorbed by the parent wing's two *Gruppen*.

AVM Leigh-Mallory had a decidedly more tentative response, establishing a 'base combat air patrol' (Base CAP) over Church Fenton, ordering Defiants (264 Sqn) to cover a 28-ship convoy steaming out of Hull, and sending 18 fighters (73 and 616 Sqns) to intercept the incoming bombers. Consequently, KG 30 pounded Driffield, wrecking four hangars and destroying ten Whitleys, badly damaging six more (77 and 102 Sqns). Only two bombers (I./KG 30) were lost in the attack, but five *Zerstörers* were shot down and two more were so badly damaged they crashed or crash-landed during their return flight. This resounding defeat deterred Luftflotte 5 from participating in any further daylight bombing missions in the campaign.

Inside a Chain Home receiver blockhouse. The receiver apparatus is on the left and the 'watch office' communications console on the right. Fortunately, none of the CH blockhouses were hit during Luftwaffe attacks. (NARA)

Adlerangriff (Eagle Attack) phase I

The main attack, 15 August 1940

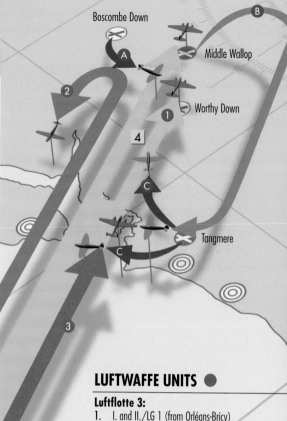

EVENTS

1. **1530–1545hrs:** following morning Stuka and Zerstörer raids that devastate Hawkinge, Lympne and Manston with little loss, Luftflotte 2 launches a large strike with 88 Do 17Zs (KG 3), escorted by 130 Bf 109s (JG 51, JG 52, JG 54) with 60 more (II. and III./JG 26) sweeping ahead of the large, wide formation. No. 11 Group responds with seven squadrons, three of which (17, 32 and 64 Sqns) are engaged by the Bf 109s and lose two Hurricanes and two Spitfires to two Bf 109s (JG 51) shot down.

2. **1545–1550hrs:** losing only two Do 17s (6./KG 3) to RAF interceptors, KG 3 strike Eastchurch (III. Gruppe) and Rochester (I. and II. Gruppen) airfields and the Short Brothers Stirling bomber factory at the latter. The airfields are devastated and Stirling production is disrupted, reducing deliveries for the next three months.

3. **1510hrs:** under cover of KG 3's large raid, ErprGr 210 flies north from Calais, at low level over open seas, to attack Martlesham Heath, a satellite field for No. 17 Squadron. Alerted late by a nearby Chain Home Low radar, that squadron scrambles one section and No. 12 Group sends 12 Spitfires (19 Sqn), but the only unit to make contact are nine Hurricanes (1 Sqn), which lose three to the Bf 109 'Jabos', and fail to score.

4. **1730–1750hrs:** Luftflotte 3 launches two major raids, simultaneously striking Portland naval base and airfields in No. 10 Group's Y-Sector. While 47 Stukas (I./StG 1 and II./StG 2) dive-bomb docks, barracks and oil storage facilities at Portland (not shown), 27 Ju 88s (I. and II./LG 1), escorted by 40 Bf 110s (II./ZG 2 and II./ZG 76) and 60 Bf 109s (JG 2), penetrate inland near Portsmouth, forcing their way through defending Hurricanes (43, 249, and 601 Sqns) and Spitfires (609 Sqn). The Bf 109 escorts return to base early due to fuel limitations and the bomber formation splits, half bombing Middle Wallop while the others hit Worthy Down and Odiham. Bombing destroys three Blenheim IFs (604 Sqn) at Middle Wallop, but losses are heavy with five Ju 88s falling to Hurricanes (601 Sqn) and two more failing to return.

5. **1830–1850hrs:** attempting to exploit Park's disrupted fighter defence, behind a large 'Freie Jagd' sweep (JG 26) Luftflotte 2 sends Staffel-strength formations of He 111s (KG 1) and Do 17s (KG 2) that hit West Malling (by mistake) and Hawkinge and the radar stations at Dover, Rye, and Foreness. Little damage is done but no losses are incurred. The sweep engages Hurricanes (151 Sqn), shooting down three for no loss.

6. **1850–1900hrs:** under the cover of the late afternoon raids, ErprGr 210 crosses the coast at Dungeness, heading north-west towards London to attack the Kenley sector station. Approaching the city's suburbs, they turn left and commence a diving attack, mistakenly, on Croydon Airport, a satellite field for No. 111 Squadron. No. 111 Squadron has just scrambled and quickly intercepts the raiders, shooting down seven 'Jabos' for no loss.

LUFTWAFFE UNITS ●

Luftflotte 3:
1. I. and II./LG 1 (from Orléans-Bricy)
2. JG 2 (from Bernay, Octeville, and Beaumont-le-Roger)
3. II./ZG 2 and II./ZG 76 (from Paris and Amiens)

Luftflotte 2:
4. KG 1 (from Amiens area)
5. KG 2 (from Arras and Cambrai)
6. KG 3 (from Antwerp and Brussels)
7. II. and III./JG 26 (fighter sweep accompanying bombers)
8. JG 51
9. JG 52
10. JG 54
11. ErprGr 210 – early raid
12. ErprGr 210 – late raid
13. I./ZG 76 (from St Omer)

KEY

RAF AMES Type 1 (long-range) 'Chain Home' Early Warning (EW) radar station

RAF Sector station

Airfield

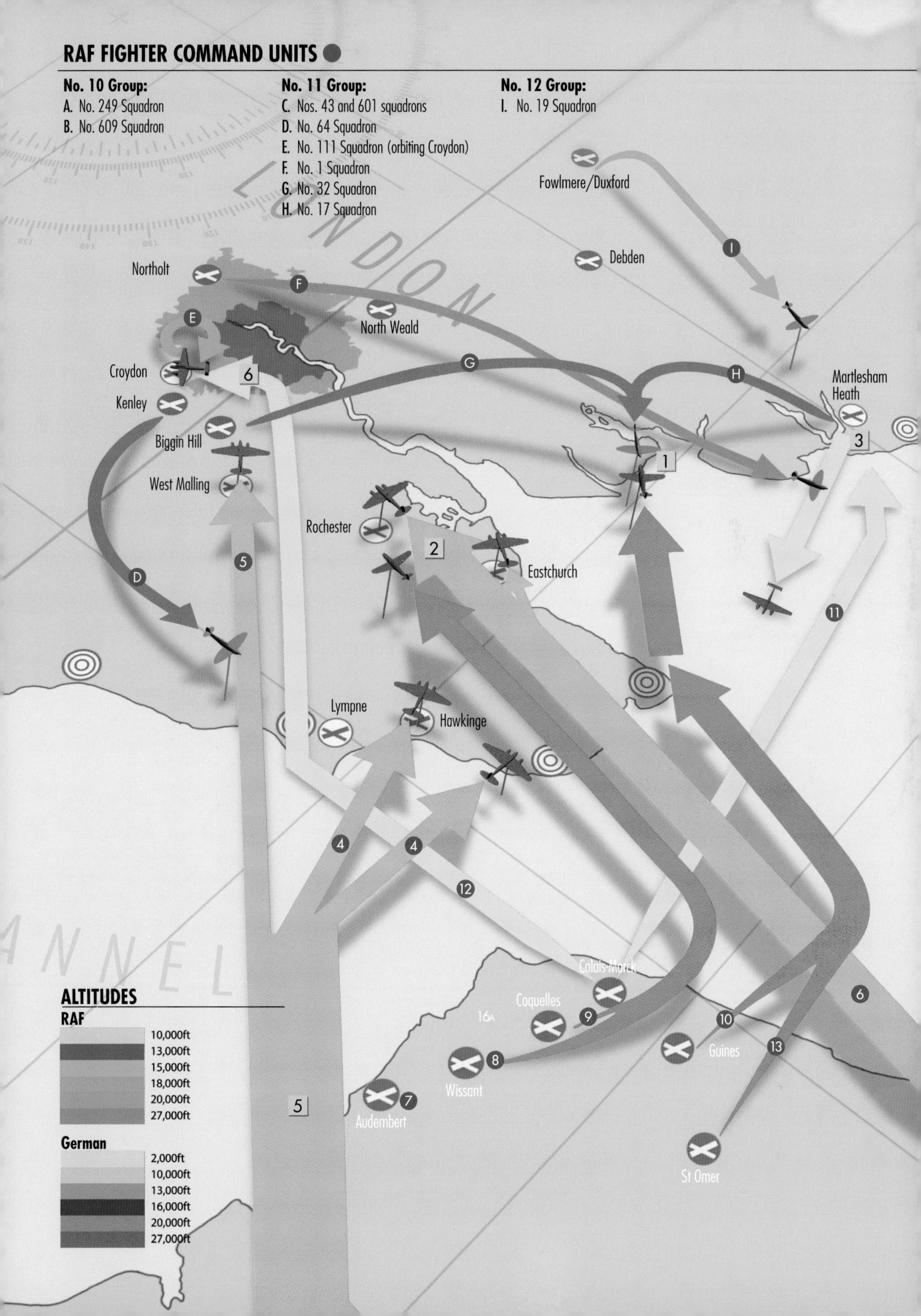

RAF FIGHTER COMMAND UNITS ●

No. 10 Group:
A. No. 249 Squadron
B. No. 609 Squadron

No. 11 Group:
C. Nos. 43 and 601 squadrons
D. No. 64 Squadron
E. No. 111 Squadron (orbiting Croydon)
F. No. 1 Squadron
G. No. 32 Squadron
H. No. 17 Squadron

No. 12 Group:
I. No. 19 Squadron

Fowlmere/Duxford

Debden

Martlesham
Heath

Northolt

North Weald

Croydon

Kenley

Biggin Hill

West Malling

Rochester

Eastchurch

Lympne

Hawkinge

London

Channel

Calais-Marck

Coquelles

Guines

Wissant

Audembert

St Omer

ALTITUDES

RAF

	10,000ft
	13,000ft
	15,000ft
	18,000ft
	20,000ft
	27,000ft

German

	2,000ft
	10,000ft
	13,000ft
	16,000ft
	20,000ft
	27,000ft

He 111H-4 1H+FS was one of eight KG 26 bombers shot down on 15 August 1940. Its crew of five were eventually rescued none the worse for wear. (Chris Goss)

16 August

Luftwaffe operations the next day continued in the same pattern as before, with Kesselring launching three small raids at around 1030hrs to prompt Park to scramble his defenders, then followed with a much larger strike an hour and a half later hoping to catch the interceptors back at their bases refuelling or rearming. Park's controllers assessed the three initial groups as feints and countered with only a few sections (three-aeroplane formations), none of which successfully intercepted. Consequently, one of the feints (III./KG 2) flew unmolested all the way to West Malling and pulverized the airfield with 80 bombs that knocked it out of action for four days.

Right on schedule, at 1145hrs, the south-eastern CH radars reported large enemy raids – approximately 300 aircraft total – approaching from the Pas de Calais. One *gruppe* of 24 Do 17s (II./KG 2) crossed Kent and followed the Thames Estuary towards Hornchurch sector station. Although intercepted (54 Sqn), none of the Dorniers were lost, but they failed to locate their target due to cloud moving in from the north. Meanwhile, a much larger force – about 150 aircraft (II./KG 1, I./KG 2, III./KG 53 and III./KG 76) – crossed the coast near Dover and was countered by 51 interceptors (32, 64, 65, 111, and 266 Sqns). The escorts successfully shielded most of their charges, but the bombers found their targets – Duxford, Debden, Hornchurch and North Weald – obscured by cloud, so they dispersed to bomb targets of opportunity: various railway stations, the Tilbury docks, Gravesend and Harwell airfields, and the RAE Farnborough.

In the now-familiar 'one-two-punch' pattern, Sperrle's main attack crossed the Channel at 1230–1250hrs, with Ju 87s (StG 2) and Bf 109s (III./JG 27) plodding along ahead of a wave of much faster Ju 88s (KG 54) and Bf 110s (III./ZG 76). AVM Brand launched four squadrons (152, 213, 234, and 249 Sqns) and Park scrambled four more (1, 43, 601, and 602 Sqns). The waves of raiders merged over the Isle of Wight and immediately split into four attack groups – most of the Stukas (I. and III./StG 2) driving straight to Tangmere before tipping over into their dives. Devastation was extensive – every hangar, the station workshops, stores, water plant, sick quarters and motor transport section were all hit. Five of FIU's seven Blenheims were destroyed, along with one Spitfire and seven Hurricanes under repair. Casualties included 20 killed and 41 injured. No. 43 Squadron Hurricanes, still climbing through lower altitudes after take-off, were perfectly positioned to attack the Ju 87s as they pulled out of their dives, quickly shooting down seven.

Meanwhile, five Stukas hit the Ventnor CH radar station with 22 bombs, knocking it out for another seven days. At nearby Bembridge, the back-up AMES Type 9(T) 40–50MHz/300kW mobile radar unit was deployed on to its 105ft tower – called a 'Remote Reserve' – but its erroneous information proved more confusing than helpful. However, the broadcast from this transmitter convinced Martini that the Ventnor radar remained operational.

The remaining *Stukagruppe* (II./StG 2) struck Royal Naval Air Station (RNAS) Lee-on-Solent, destroying three hangars and six aircraft, killing 14 people. Additionally, the Ju 88s struck RNAS Gosport, doing some damage and killing six servicemen – 234 Squadron was vectored to intercept, but failed to find the raiders. No. 249 attempted to engage the escorting *Zerstörers* but was bounced instead by Bf 109s, which shot down two of them; the pilot of one, Flight Lieutenant James Nicolson, was awarded Fighter Command's only Victoria Cross under rather confounded circumstances.

Luftflotte 3's second attack – He 111s from four *Kampfgruppen* (I. and II./KG 27 and II. and III./KG 55) – crossed the coast near Brighton just after 1700hrs and were soon intercepted by five squadrons (1, 32, 64, 601, and 615 Sqns), while two more (234 and 602 Sqns) engaged a *freie Jagd* sweep over the Isle of Wight. The result was a classic large-scale air battle in which eight Heinkels were shot down and, for the first time on a major scale, the raids were broken up.

While most of the raiders were turned back, a pair of He 111s (3./KG 27) continued, descending below the expansive undercast, looking for targets of opportunity. Arriving at the landing circuit at Brize Norton airfield (mistaking it for RAF Benson), they lowered their undercarriages to fool the local AA gunners, then, suddenly, they raised their wheels, accelerated at full power, and dumped 32 bombs into the base's hangars. The resulting explosions and conflagration destroyed 11 Hurricanes under repair by No. 6 Maintenance Unit and 35 twin-engined Airspeed Oxford trainers.

For the second day in a row, the two Luftflotten had launched more than 1,700 sorties against airfield targets in southern England; Tangmere was badly hit and five others

Typically, each morning the Luftwaffe's dedicated reconnaissance aircraft, such as the new Dornier Do 217, would range across England, photographing RAF airfields. If quick development of the films indicated a large number of aircraft at a particular aerodrome, then that airfield would usually be added to the target list for the day. (NARA)

The low altitude attack on RAF Kenley by 9./KG 76's Do 17Zs suffered heavy losses – four bombers shot down, two badly damaged, and 16 aircrew killed, captured, or wounded. (Private Collection)

were damaged, destroying 20 day fighters and eight Blenheim IFs on the ground, while 19 Hurricanes and Spitfires were shot down. Fifteen Bf 109s were lost, making the day's 'exchange rate' close to even. Additionally, 11 bombers had been lost to Dowding's interceptors. The Luftwaffe's success this day was moderate, but the costs were increasing; most disturbing was the day's loss of nine Stukas and eight *Zerstörers*.

After two days at full cry, the extensive sheets of low clouds moving into southern England precluded effective operations the following day and only 77 sorties were mounted, with negligible results and no losses to either side.

18 August

After a day to rest and regroup, Luftflotten 2 and 3 returned to the battle with renewed vigour. While Sperrle's Luftlotte 3 continued to batter the coastal airfields around Portsmouth and Southampton in preparation for Operation *Seelöwe*, Kesselring's mission planners moved the fight inland, targeting the sector stations at Kenley and Biggin Hill. Recent photo reconnaissance and signals intercepts had revealed that these two were the RAF's major fighter bases covering the proposed invasion beaches in south-east England and, having devastated the 'satellite airfields' nearer the coast, it was time to launch major strikes against the main bases. Following the usual operational and weather reconnaissance – and after a delay due to heavy cloud over northern France – Luftflotte 2 launched its main effort shortly after midday.

A *Schwarm* (four-fighter formation) of Bf 109Es from 1./JG 3 on a *freie Jagd* sweep. (NARA)

Behind a *freie Jagd* sweep of 60 Bf 109s (III./JG 3 and III./JG 26), the bombers were organized in two 'packages', each consisting of three parts. Leading the strike were to be 12 Ju 88s (II./KG 76) dive-bombing Kenley's hangars and buildings, followed by 27 Do 17s (I. and III./KG 76), with nine more Dorniers providing a follow-up attack at low level. However, delays and disruptions due to weather resulted in the formations crossing the Straits of Dover in the opposite order, the low-level Dorniers leading, with the whole operation covered by an additional 350 'Emils' and 73 *Zerstörers*. Unescorted, unhindered by the clouds (8/10ths coverage at 6,500–10,000ft over the Pas de Calais) and unseen by radar, 9./KG 76's nine Do 17s raced across the waters at low level, making landfall near Beachy Head. Observer Corps posts reported their progress as they followed the Brighton–London railway line leading to Kenley. Five minutes behind KG 76's other 39 bombers came 60 He 111s (KGs 1 and 27), also at medium altitude – flying in three *gruppe*-strength waves, escorted by 40 Bf 109s (JG 54) – headed for Biggin Hill.

The large formations of bombers were first detected by the Swingate CH radar just after noon and after about 45 minutes the large, ill-defined 'echo' resolved into six groups, staggered in range. No. 11 Group's controllers responded by positioning five squadrons (53 interceptors) to patrol the Canterbury–Margate line at 20,000ft to protect port facilities along the Thames Estuary and airfields north of it, scrambled four more (50 interceptors) to CAP over the two sector stations and had six more in 'readiness' (to be airborne in five minutes). Once the bombers crossed the coast, a heavy haze layer above 4,000ft prevented the Observer Corps from accurately tracking them as they outflanked the patrol line to the south while the fighter sweep engaged the southernmost interceptor squadron (501 Sqn), shooting down four without loss.

At 1322hrs Kenley was hit first by the low-flying 9. Staffel, which lost four Dorniers shot down and two others badly damaged, with 16 of the 40 aircrew (including all the officers) killed, wounded, or captured, then five minutes later by the medium-level bombers. The smoke and debris thrown into the air dissuaded the Ju 88s from dive-bombing and they struck West Malling instead. Kenley was devastated; three hangars were demolished, the station HQ wrecked, two messes and other buildings damaged, ten Hurricanes and two Blenheims were destroyed, and 32 personnel killed or injured. Exploding bombs severed underground cables, cutting communications with No. 11 Group HQ and all other outside agencies; it took 60 hours to fully restore communications. Eventually the Sector Operations Room was moved into an empty butcher's shop in Caterham where it was 'tied into' nearby General Post Office (GPO) telephone lines. The Base CAP shot down four of the 39 level bombers.

On 18 August, Luftflotte 3 launched the largest Stuka attack of the campaign, striking three airfields and the Poling CH radar station. Sixteen of the 109 Ju 87s were shot down. (Getty/Keystone)

Protected by nothing but perspex panes and cramped in the small confines of Luftwaffe bomber cockpits, aircrew suffered high casualties to Hurricane and Spitfire rifle-calibre machine gun fire. (NARA)

The three waves of He 111s (I./KG 1 and II. and III./KG 27) attacked Biggin Hill, where most of the 84 tons of bombs fell upon the landing grounds and in the woods east of the airfield. However, here too, communications were cut and for more than two hours No. 11 Group had no control of airborne interceptors in B- and C-Sectors; six squadrons recovered to whatever airfield they could find, most of which lacked contact with Fighter Command.

As Luftflotte 2's bombs were falling, around Cherbourg the first of 109 Ju 87s began taking off from their forward airfields. It was the largest Stuka strike of the campaign: four *gruppen* (StG 77 and I./StG 3) launching at 1330hrs to follow a *freie Jagd* sweep of 55 Bf 109s (JG 2) and escorted by 102 more (JG 27 and I./JG 53). Each *Stukagruppe* was assigned a separate target – Coastal Command's Thorney Island base, RNAS Ford and RNAS Gosport, and the Poling CH station. That radar detected the first 'echos' of the plodding strike force at 1359hrs, just as the four *Jagdgruppen* reached their escort positions. Brand and Park launched three squadrons each, totalling 45 Spitfires and 23 Hurricanes and, from Thorney Island, 235 Squadron launched a flight of Blenheim IVF long-range maritime fighters.

At 1420hrs the huge formation of Stukas arrived over Selsey Bill and split, each *gruppe* heading for its target, accompanied by their escorts. Ford, Gosport and Poling were all hit before the RAF interceptors could engage. Ford was devastated: the fuel dump was set alight and two hangars, motor transport (MT), stores, and several buildings were damaged. Twelve biplane torpedo bombers (829 Naval Air Squadron) were destroyed and 26 other aircraft demolished; 28 people were killed and 75 injured. The base was knocked out of action until the navy evacuated and turned it over to the RAF the next month. Gosport had two hangars damaged, several buildings wrecked, and four aircraft destroyed.

The Poling CH radar was knocked out when a bomb took the top off one of the receiver masts. A 'Remote Reserve' was erected, but was of limited use – it took a week to restore the CH to full operation.

Thorney Island was also hit hard – two hangars and several buildings were wrecked, three aircraft destroyed – but the raiders (I./StG 77) were intercepted by 18 Hurricanes (43 and 601 Sqns) and lost ten Stukas shot down and 28 aircrew killed, captured, and wounded. The Spitfire squadrons chased the retiring Stukas 18 miles out to sea, shooting down six more.

Luftflotte 2's late afternoon raid planned to hit the sector stations at Hornchurch and North Weald with 58 Dorniers (KG 2) and 51 Heinkels (KG 53) respectively, escorted by 140 Bf 109s and 110s (elements of JG 3, 26, 51 and 54, and ZG 26). The two formations, separated by 15 minutes, gathered their escorts over the Pas de Calais and headed north past Dover before turning inland. They were first detected at about 1700hrs, and the D-Sector controller positioned four squadrons (44 interceptors) on the Canterbury–Margate patrol line while Park launched four more (49 interceptors) to Base CAPs and called two more to readiness – a total of 143 aeroplanes was eventually launched. The raiders found their objectives blanketed by thick cloud at 5,000–10,000ft and turned back to bomb their secondary targets: the army barracks at Shoeburyness and the Royal Marine barracks at Deal. The abort spoilt the defenders' intercepts and only two He 111s were lost.

Overall, the two Luftflotten flew approximately 750 offensive daytime sorties (and another 170 that night), while Fighter Command had countered with 886 interceptor sorties, of which 403 engaged the raiders, their escorts or fighter sweeps. They shot down 14 bombers, 16 Stukas, 15 *Zerstörers*, and 18 Bf 109s – a total of 63 warplanes. However, the Luftflottens' aggressive airfield attacks destroyed 19 RAF aircraft – including eight interceptors – and 12 RN torpedo bombers, while another 34 Spitfires and Hurricanes were lost in aerial combat.

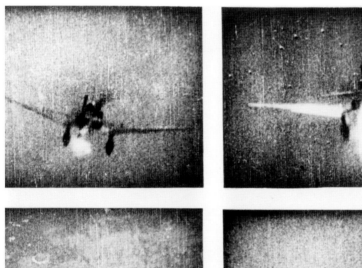
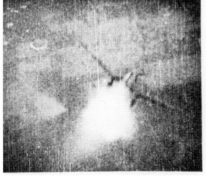

The chronically slow, fixed-undercarriage *Stuka* was extremely vulnerable to fighter attack, resulting in the loss of 67 total (21.5 per cent of initial strength) in the entire campaign. (IWM C 2418)

Unable to fulfil its role as the Luftwaffe's bomber escort fighter, the Bf 110 *Zerstörer* was ordered to be used only when bomber missions planned to exceed the Bf 109's limited range and flying post-strike *freie Jagd* sweeps to cover egressing formations. (Private Collection)

Adlerangriff Phase II: 24 August–6 September

We have reached the decisive period in the air war against England. The vital task is to turn all means at our disposal to the defeat of the enemy air force. Our first aim is the destruction of enemy fighters. If they no longer take to the air, we shall attack them on the ground, or force them into battle by directing our bombers against targets within range of our fighters.

Hermann Göring, Meeting with Luftwaffe commanders and ObdL staff officers, Carinhall, 19 August 1940

In preparation for Göring's next commanders' conference at Carinhall, Schmid composed an intelligence assessment that glowingly trumpeted the Luftwaffe's successful accomplishment of *Adlerangriff's* Phase I. He reported that 'eight major air bases… [have been] virtually destroyed'. In fact, photographic reconnaissance seemed to confirm that 'the bulk of Fighter Command has withdrawn to the capital's [London's] environs.' By this time, Martini's *Funkhorchdienst* had pinpointed six locations – all on airfields within 50km of London's outskirts – from which RAF fighter squadrons were being directed to intercept incoming raids. In light of the difficulty in bringing down the coastal radar aerial towers, he recommended these be targeted.

Moreover, accepting *Jagdwaffe* 'victory claims' as fact, Schmid assessed that 551 RAF fighters (of 823 aircraft total) had been destroyed since 1 July. Compared with the loss of 127 Bf 109Es during the same period, this gave the 'Emil' a perceived 4.5:1 'kill ratio', encouraging increased fighter-vs-fighter combat as a prescription for further success. (The actual number of Hurricanes and Spitfires lost in combat from July 1 to August 16 was 214.) By subtracting this over-estimate from his initial tabulation (his 16 July assessment stated '900 first-line fighters available, of which approximately 675 may be regarded as operational' – Dowding actually had 901 total available, 666 in combat units on 13 July) and adding back his under-estimated Spitfire and Hurricane production, he derived a deluded and deceptively optimistic estimate that Fighter Command had only 430 day fighters remaining, of which approximately 330 were thought to be in southern England.

This perceived success had come at an alarming cost. During the nearly week-long offensive thus far, the Luftwaffe had lost 297 aircraft on combat operations – which was a troubling increase of almost 600 per cent, up drastically from the 204 losses sustained during *Kanalkampf's* preceding six weeks (1 July through 11 August, a weekly average of 34). Ever a politician, the Luftwaffe was Göring's primary power base and the source of his prestige and position within the leadership of the Third Reich. Win or lose, he could not afford to see it heavily eroded in accomplishing its mission, so the theme of the *Besprechung* was to reduce the unacceptable loss rates as much as possible.

Some 127 light and medium bombers (12.7 per cent of those serviceable on 13 August) and 52 Stukas (16.7 per cent of strength) had been lost to RAF interceptors and ground-based defences. While bomber losses had been readily replaced with new aircraft, combat damage had reduced serviceability to 70 per cent. Far more critical were aircrew losses, which included 172 officers – including two KG *Kommodoren*, two Fliegerkorps COSs, and seven *Gruppenkommandeure*. This sort of haemorrhaging had to stop if the Luftwaffe was to survive its anticipated victory.

To facilitate this, the campaign's overall aim would remain unchanged, but the focus and the operational strategy were to be different. For focus, rather than attack RAF (and RN) installations in general, Göring directed that, specifically, for daylight missions Fighter Command bases were to be targeted to 'force them into battle by directing bomber attacks against targets within range of our fighters'. And the operational strategy was to become one of attrition warfare in fighter-vs-fighter combat.

The attendees agreed that bomber formations larger than *gruppe*-strength could not be adequately protected, so, instead of Phase I's *Kampfgeschwader*-strength (two or three *gruppen*) raids, smaller bomber formations were to be used. Göring emphasized that

No. 264 Squadron joined the battle on 24 August and over the next five days lost ten Defiants shot down and another seven damaged. Having shot down only six German bombers, the squadron and its last five 'turret fighters' were transferred north to Kirton-in-Lindsey where the unit became a night fighter squadron. (IWM CH 884)

At the end of August, *Oberst* Robert Fuchs led his two-*gruppen* strong KG 26 *Löwe* ('Lion') bomber wing from Norway to Holland and Belgium to resume participation in the ongoing offensive, reinforcing I. *Fliegerkorps* with 57 He 111H medium bombers. (NARA)

'bombers were to be used only in sufficient numbers to draw up British fighters.' The bombers' close escort would continue to consist of three *Jagdgruppen*, but Göring stressed that the maximum number of fighters should be sent on *freie Jagd* missions, saying:

> Only part of the fighters are to be employed as direct escorts to our bombers. The aim must be to employ the strongest possible fighter forces on free-hunt operations in which they can indirectly protect the bombers, and at the same time come to grips under favourable conditions with enemy fighters.

Consequently, twice as many fighters were needed to escort and sweep for bomber formations than had previously been used. With the geographical focus of the campaign shifting from the initial, broad, 280-mile wide front to the concentration on defeating Fighter Command's No. 11 Group (a 165-mile front), all Luftflotte 3's 'Emils' were ordered transferred to Luftflotte 2, beginning on 22 August.

Additionally, Göring directed that attacks against 'the ground organisation of the enemy bombers [must be] conducted in such a manner as to avoid all unnecessary losses' – which meant night attacks – and that British aircraft industries were to be attacked only by individual or small groups of bombers operating in bad weather or at night. Since the high ratio of fighters to bombers limited Luftflotte 2 to fewer than 300 bombing sorties per day, by the end of the month I. Fliegerkorps was transferred to Sperrle, as had already the special radio-bombing KGr 100. Following an abortive daylight attack on Portsmouth on 26 August, Luftflotte 3 began a concerted night bombing offensive against Bomber Command bases, major ports, industrial areas, and other strategic targets.

The Stuka force had to be preserved for its primary role: providing close air support for the Wehrmacht's cross-Channel offensive. In any event, the Ju 87's limited range and its special requirement for a permissive operating environment (local air supremacy) precluded its participation in missions that penetrated deeper into fighter-contested airspace. Consequently, Göring directed 'Until the enemy fighter force has been broken, Stuka units are only to be used when circumstances are particularly favourable.'

To facilitate this decision, on 29 August ObdL transferred von Richthofen's VIII Fliegerkorps to Luftflotte 2, where Kesselring held it in abeyance for *Seelöwe*. The withdrawal of the Stukas was balanced somewhat by the arrival of II.(Schlact)/LG 2, which had just completed the four-week conversion from the Henschel Hs 123 'assault' biplane to the new Bf 109E-7 *Jabo*. Arriving in late August, this new unit doubled Kesselring's fighter-bomber strike force.

Finally, there was the unsatisfactory situation with the Bf 110 *Zerstörer*. With an alarming 53 aircraft (20.15 per cent of strength) lost, it was now obvious that the type was patently unsuited for its intended role. Nonetheless, Göring directed 'Twin-engine fighters are to be employed where the range of single-engine fighters is insufficient, or where they can facilitate the breaking-off from combat of single-engine formations.' The *Jagdwaffe* remained healthy with 65 'Emils' (seven per cent of the force) lost during Phase I, having shot down 114 RAF interceptors during this period (1.75:1 'kill ratio'), and with losses rapidly replaced and 85 per cent serviceability in frontline units. In addition to receiving JG 27 and JG 53 from Sperrle, Luftflotte 2 was reinforced with I./JG 77 from Luftflotte 5.

24–29 August

The movement of nine *Jagdgruppen* required several days, and this – plus four days of cloudy weather – resulted in delaying renewed operations until 24 August, when Phase II began with some 1,030 sorties. Many of these were large formations of fighters flying along the English coast, about 20 miles offshore, and feinting inland, to screen gathering formations from Park's EW radars. Under cover of these screens and feints, two mid-morning *freie Jagd* missions were followed by a major midday raid – 40 Do 17Zs and Ju 88As (KG 76) escorted by 66 Bf 109Es (JG 3 and 26) – that attacked Dover (as a feint) and Manston. Twelve squadrons were scrambled but only two managed to break through the fighter screen, with 264 Squadron Defiants destroying four Junkers before JG 3 'Emils' and Ju 88As' return

WAAF 'plotters' at work in the Operations Room at HQ No. 11 Group, RAF Uxbridge. Although this scene appears relaxed, during the most intense air battles the plotters, tellers, and controllers were overwhelmed with information. (IWM CH 7698)

fire shot down four of the 'turret fighters'. The battered airfield was devastated yet again, destroying the living quarters, causing 17 casualties and badly damaging three aircraft.

Kesselring's second wave launched mid-afternoon with 46 heavily escorted He 111s (KG 53) flying up the Thames Estuary to attack Hornchurch and North Weald. Park's D-Sector controller vectored four squadrons (56, 111, 151 and 615 Sqns) to intercept – the defenders shooting down five of the raiders – and called No. 12 Group to provide coverage for the two bases. Leigh-Mallory's units failed to show up and left the bases exposed. Twenty Heinkels pounded North Weald, causing 19 casualties, destroying station buildings, married quarters and stores, and damaging the power station. Hornchurch was also hit, though less badly, and 264 Squadron lost three more Defiants during its scramble.

Under cover of this large raid coming in at 12,000ft, ErprGr 210 hit Manston in yet another classic low-altitude attack. This raid severed all communications with Uxbridge, finally causing Dowding to withdraw 600 Squadron to Hornchurch and, evacuating everyone except ground defence and servicing personnel, to designate the wrecked airfield as an 'emergency landing ground'.

From 25 to 29 August, operations continued at a lesser pace, averaging 700 sorties daily, with many of these being screening missions. Five sector stations were targeted but, due mainly to bad weather, only the Debden strike (by I./KG 2) was successful, along with raids on 'satellite airfields' at Eastchurch, Rochford, and Warmwell. While the new strategy was successful in reducing bomber losses, it was not as effective in destroying British fighters as was hoped, primarily because Park's controllers held back airborne squadrons unless they determined that the target formation was bombers, not a fighter sweep. Since No. 11 Group judiciously and obstinately avoided fighter-vs-fighter engagements, in the second week of this phase Kesselring's mission planners sought to relentlessly threaten Park's six main bases. To provide fresh units for these attacks, the two Luftflotten were reinforced with the arrival of KG 26 and KG 30 from Luftflotte 5, as well as the return of KG 77, which had just completed its conversion to the Ju 88.

During this period the Luftwaffe's night bombing effort doubled to as many as 170 sorties per night. The increased effort had an inauspicious beginning, however, when, on the evening of 24/25 August, a wayward He 111 – while attempting to bomb the oil storage facilities at Rochester and Thameshaven – overshot its target in bad weather and dumped its load of bombs on the East Ham and Bethnal Green boroughs of London. Churchill immediately authorized a retaliatory strike by Bomber Command, which sent 81 twin-engine medium bombers to Berlin the very next night. Bad weather foiled this initial attack: only ten bombers reached Berlin's outskirts and these unloaded their bombs on the city's municipal farms. But this raid was followed by moderately more successful strikes on 28/29 and 29/30 August, which resulted in Hitler lifting the ban on bombing London the following day.

The Battle of Biggin Hill: 30 August–6 September

Word of Hitler's decision spread quickly and Göring scheduled another commanders' conference for 3 September in The Hague to 'hammer out' the details of implementing a new operations strategy. In the meantime, to 'pave the way' on the direct route between the Pas de Calais and London, the No. 11 Group sector station at Biggin Hill became the primary target. C-Sector covered a 45-mile front along the coast from Hastings to Folkestone and, if this base could be neutralized, London could be assaulted repeatedly with, hopefully, much lower losses.

An expansive anti-cyclone weather system had settled into north-west Europe, clearing English skies of the clouds that had inhibited the past four days of operations, promising fine weather for the next several days. Taking advantage of clear skies and the recently arrived reinforcements, Luftflotte 2 planned a renewed offensive with a record number of sorties for its command (1,345) and changed tactics. Instead of sending two or three large waves of bombers, each in tightly spaced 'packages', Kesselring's planners began launching almost continuous streams of smaller-sized raids at 20- or 30-minute intervals across a three- to four-hour period. The intent was to saturate No. 11 Group's command and control capability over time rather than attempt to overwhelm them all at once.

Luftflotte 2 hit Biggin Hill twice the first day. Behind a 60-fighter *freie Jagd* sweep crossing the Kent coast at 1030hrs and a force of 140 bombers and fighters following half an hour later, about noon a *staffel* of Ju 88As hit the sector station unopposed. The new tactics worked – by 1145hrs all Park's interceptors were airborne and ten squadrons were engaged, making the raid situation over Kent so confused the controllers lost track of which enemy formations had been intercepted. The Junkers dropped more than 30 delayed-action SC 250 bombs from 18,000ft altitude, but – typically – accuracy was wanting and the rain of high explosive was scattered across the villages of Keston and Biggin Hill as well as the landing grounds.

The second raid used the late afternoon third wave – primarily consisting of 60 He 111s (II./KG 1 and I. and II./KG 53) hitting the Vauxhall motor works at Luton and the Handley Page factory at Radlett – as cover to conduct another 'snap attack'. This one was flown by the indomitable ErprGr 210 using ten Bf 110Ds to lead a half-dozen Bf 109E-7 *Jabos* from II.(S)/LG 2 on their very first operational mission. The attackers came in fast and low, dropping 16 SC 250 and SC 500 bombs on hangars, buildings, and other structures. One hangar – and a Hurricane (32 Sqn) inside – was destroyed, as were the MT pool, station workshops, armoury, and stores; sergeants' mess and WAAF quarters; and NAAFI and cookhouse. Telephone/telegraph lines and the electricity, gas, and water mains were all cut, and 39 personnel were killed with another 26 wounded. C-Sector control went 'off the air',

Battle of Biggin Hill

As Luftflotte 2's concentration on RAF Sector Stations took priority, Biggin Hill was attacked twice on 30 August. The second, a late afternoon low-level *Jabo* attack by ten ErprGr 210 Bf 110s and six Bf 109s, devastated the base's 'North Camp', demolishing one large hangar, aircraft workshops, stores and motor transport yard, armoury and guardroom, and barracks and a bomb shelter – killing 39 personnel and wounding 26 more. Gas, water and electrical lines were severed and the telecommunications cables were cut in three places. While Hornchurch took over controlling intercepts in C-Sector, the communications lines were repaired overnight and the base was back 'on-line' the next morning.

Next day Biggin Hill was hit again at 1300hrs by Do 17Zs that bombed 'South Camp' from 12,000ft, destroying that side's large hangar and damaging the married quarters, messes and NAAFI facility. Two hours later, led by Sqn Ldr A. R. Collings, No. 72 Squadron landed 21 Spitfire Mk IAs, flying from Acklington to replace the badly-depleted and just-departed 610 Squadron. The fresh squadron was immediately refuelled and placed on 20-minute 'Available' status and, at 1745hrs, 'Tennis Squadron' (their radio call sign) was scrambled to meet the next wave of raiders. Twenty Spitfires were launched and vectored south-east to intercept I./KG 3 Do 17Zs north-west of Dungeness – shooting down one but losing two to escorting Bf 109Es.

While they were away, at 1800hrs a *Staffel* of Do 17Zs from III./KG 76 made a low altitude strike unopposed. No. 79 Squadron (call sign 'Pansy') scrambled immediately, launching all six of its serviceable Hurricanes climbing hard to catch the departing Dorniers, only to lose two to escorting Bf 109Es.

The 'North Camp' was once again hit hard, wrecking the large 3-Bay hangar and scoring a direct hit on the Sector Operations Block, again severing the tattered, patched together communications lines. In the dispersal area, 72 Squadron's one unserviceable Spitfire (R6928; believed to be coded RN●N   ) remained – but not for long. The aeroplane could not be fixed in time to scramble, so the pilot, Sgt R. C. J. Staples, and ground crew dived into the nearby 'slit trench' with a Lewis machine gun team as the bombs began 'crumping' across the airfield and crashing into the buildings and hangars of 'North Camp'.

According to airframe-fitter Corporal Graeme Gillard, 'From our bomb shelter we saw our lone unserviceable Spitfire just curling up under the bombardment. One of our electricians, a brave but silly man, ran out to pick up an unexploded bomb. It exploded halfway to the perimeter woods. Many casualties, mostly WAAF, occurred. The runway was out of action.'

Although considered slow and obsolescent, Dornier Do 17Z light bombers carried the brunt of the Luftwaffe's offensive, especially in attacks against the Sector Stations and other airfields. Frequently caught by the speedier Spitfires and Hurricanes, several units suffered heavily, especially when egressing from the target areas. (NARA)

but Hornchurch (D-Sector) took over until power and communications could be restored. The attackers escaped without loss.

The confused 'air picture' over south-east England was made even worse by a reportedly 'lucky hit' on Kent's main electricity grid during the morning attacks. It cut power to the CH radars at Pevensey, Rye, and Swingate – along with four interspersed CHL stations – opening an 80-mile wide gap in Park's EW radar net. Martini's *Funkhorchdienst* recognized that the radars went 'down' and Kesselring's planners sought to take advantage of this for the next day's missions.

Following the obligatory early morning fighter sweep that Park's controllers largely ignored, at about 0800hrs some 200 bombers and fighters were detected by the Dunkirk (Canterbury) and Canewdon CH radars, approaching via the Thames Estuary. Park scrambled 13 squadrons to intercept three *staffel*-strength formations, heavily escorted by Bf 110s. These split up to attack North Weald, Debden, and – for the first and only time in the campaign – the No. 12 Group sector station of Duxford (III./KG 2), while a smaller force following an hour later hit Eastchurch. Meanwhile, along the south-east coast, power had finally been restored to the EW radar net, just in time to be attacked by ErprGr 210, which bombed the CH radars at Pevensey, Rye, and Swingate and three CHL sites, knocking them out for the rest of the day.

The midday wave of raiders hit Croydon, Hornchurch, and Biggin Hill. Showing the emphasis that the latter had drawn, Biggin Hill was bombed from 12,000ft by a two-*staffel gruppe* of Do 17s (KG 2), cratering the landing grounds and damaging another hangar, married quarters, messes, and the Sector Operations Room. Once again the raiders departed without loss.

Both Hornchurch and Biggin Hill were attacked again in the late afternoon. The latter is believed to have been struck by III./KG 76, the Do 17-flying low-altitude airfield attack specialists. They destroyed another large hangar, a Spitfire (72 Sqn) in the dispersal area, and hit the Sector Operations building. All telephone lines were severed, once again cutting off contact with Uxbridge until they could be repaired, forcing Kenley (B-Sector) to take over control of C-Sector. Once again the raiders egressed without loss.

Of the day's 1,451 sorties – a new record – only 150 were bombers. These were protected by 1,301 fighter sorties, which limited actual RAF victories (in spite of much higher claims) to only eight bombers, while 25 Hurricanes and eight Spitfires were shot down in exchange for 19 Bf 109s and six *Zerstörers* shot down. Additionally, seven Fighter Command bases – five of them sector stations – had been bombed, two of them twice, destroying six Spitfires on the ground. Another record was set this day: at 39, Fighter Command suffered its highest losses of the campaign. It certainly looked like the Luftwaffe had finally got it right.

The 640 sorties flown on 1 September included three attacks on Biggin Hill, with other raids against Debden, Kenley (which missed), Eastchurch, Hawkinge, Lympne, and Detling. The last attack launched against Biggin Hill at 1730hrs – one group of Dorniers and six of Bf 109s sweeping ahead. Park's controllers, believing them to all to be fighter formations, refused combat, allowing the bombers to strike their target unopposed. This raid virtually completed the destruction of the base, scoring a direct hit on the Sector Operations building. The landing grounds were unusable, practically all buildings were uninhabitable, and all communications in and off the base were once again severed, forcing many of the station's sections to move into nearby Keston village. No. 72 Squadron had been moved to Croydon that morning, where it was now assigned to B-Sector – it

Fighter Command suffered its worst losses on 31 August, losing 39 Hurricanes and Spitfires in aerial combat and from bombing attacks on airfields. (NARA)

would not return to Biggin Hill until 12 September. With its five serviceable Hurricanes, 79 Squadron became a 'local base defence flight'. While intercepting the second raid, two of these Hurricanes were shot down – both pilots survived wounded and burned – and the third crashed upon landing. The sector's third unit – 501 Squadron stationed at the Gravesend 'satellite field' – was reassigned to D-Sector for over a week.

Meanwhile, C-Sector Operations Room was moved to a vacant shop in Pantiles, half a mile south of the airfield. GPO technicians worked through the night tying into the nearby main telephone/telegraph lines, building a switchboard, and reconstructing the Sector Operations Room. Although contact was re-established within three hours, even limited fighter control capability was not restored until the next morning.

Biggin Hill was attacked four times in the next four days – along with Hornchurch (twice), North Weald, Gravesend, Eastchurch, and Detling – but by then there was really nothing left to bomb. Sector stations Kenley and Debden and two other fighter bases had also been battered into degraded operations. The primary impact was the repeated cutting of 'landline' communications between Uxbridge, Sector Stations, and Observer Posts, placing some of Park's Spitfire and Hurricane squadrons at an untimely disadvantage. However, overall, Fighter Command's IADS had proven exceptionally resilient to the repeated battering; even when one particular and strategically located Sector Station was beaten into submission, the system compensated for degraded operations and Britain's air defence was never seriously compromised.

For *Adlerangriff* Phase II, Göring had established three objectives: 1.) reduce bomber losses to sustainable levels, and neutralize Fighter Command by 2.) bombing Dowding's

Major Adolf Galland, the 28-year-old commander of JG 26 and one of the top scoring Luftwaffe aces of the campaign, demonstrates how he 'bagged' his latest kill. In general, the consistently high *Jagdwaffe* 'victory claims' – averaging 2.5 to 3.3 times RAF losses – encouraged a crucial and fateful shift in operational strategy. (NMUSAF)

interceptors on the ground and 3.) causing high attrition in fighter-vs-fighter combat. Certainly the revised operational strategy was successful in meeting the first aim: during the fortnight of daylight bombing missions, only 68 bombers were lost in combat, reducing losses to their pre-*Adlertag* level. However, the concentrated attacks against airfields destroyed only 15 interceptors (including one Blenheim) because of Fighter Command's robust air raid warning system and the practice of 'survival scrambling' unserviceable but airworthy aircraft to orbit or land north of the battle areas. Finally, the attrition in air-to-air combat was not as high as expected either: Dowding lost 244 day fighters in this two-week period, 208 of them to Bf 109s (which lost 150). Despite the 'Emil's' continued favourable 'kill ratio' (now 1.4:1), Fighter Command's operational strength remained steady with 358 operational day fighters due to the timely arrivals of replacements.

On 30 August OKH issued the final version of the army's *Seelöwe* invasion plan and four days later OKW issued the operations order that established the timetable for execution: the navy's ship loading and mine-laying were to begin on 12 September with '*S-Tag*' ('Sea Lion Day', the German equivalent of 'D-Day') set for 21 September. Now feeling the pressure to force *Adlerangriff* to a favourable conclusion – Göring actually hoped 'his Luftwaffe' would force the British to capitulate – the *Reichsmarschall* called for yet another conference, held on 3 September at The Hague, to determine how to win the campaign through air power alone.

Adlerangriff Phase III: 7–30 September

We have no chance of destroying the English fighters on the ground. We must force their last reserves… into combat in the air.

Hermann Göring, Meeting with Luftflotte commanders, The Hague, 3 September, 1940

Anticipating Göring's commanders' conference at The Hague, ObdL Intelligence prepared another periodic assessment of the RAF. Using his previous rubric, Schmid assessed:

In the battle for air superiority the RAF since August 8th has lost 1,115 fighters… However, a large number of British aircraft claimed by us as destroyed can in fact be made serviceable very quickly. [Additionally] Eighteen aerodromes [have been] destroyed and another 26 damaged.

However, considering Fighter Command's continued active defence, he upgraded his current strength estimates. Suggesting that the week-long hiatus (18–24 August, while *Jagdwaffe* units were moved and bad weather occurred) allowed British aircraft production to make good its losses, in his second 'uptick' in as many weeks, Schmid estimated Fighter Command strength on 1 September to be '600 fighter planes, of which 420 were [stationed in south-east England], and a reserve of 100 in the factories [awaiting delivery].' (Actually on 6/7 September, including Defiants and Blenheims, Dowding had 746 fighters on strength [548 serviceable] with 127 in 'ready reserve' and 160 'nearly finished' at the factories. On 7 September, the two Luftflotten had 623 operational Bf 109Es, of 787 total.)

The day following the RAF's 29/30 August raid on Berlin, Hitler authorized 'reprisal attacks on London,' provided they would not be *Terrorangriff* ('terror attacks') against

residential areas. Codenaming the new target as *Loge* (the ancient Norse giant god of fire), Göring saw this as an opportunity to win – and end – the conflict by forcing British capitulation, in tandem with pursuing the operational aim of attaining air superiority over south-east England by increased fighter-vs-fighter combat.

Göring and his ObdL staff now realized – through the Luftflotten's diligent though sketchy morning photo-reconnaissance of RAF airfields – that few British aircraft were being destroyed on the ground. The resulting photographs showed landing grounds pocked with scores of craters, but there were disappointingly few tell-tale scorch marks signifying burnt aircraft wreckage. The only aspect of the campaign that seemed to be working (based on exaggerated victory claims) was the *Jagdwaffe*'s air-to-air combat. Göring, whose only military experience was as a World War I fighter pilot, seized upon this as the solution. The need to defend London was sure to draw Dowding's 'last 50 Spitfires' (Göring's words) into battle, where the *Jagdwaffe*'s seemingly advantageous 'kill ratio' would prove decisive. However, to avoid any appearance of noncompliance with Hitler's caveat, in accordance with Hitler's 1 August Directive No. 17, only the London East End docks would be targeted.

7 September

With great fanfare, Göring arrived at Cap Blanc Nez to watch 'his Luftwaffe' stream overhead towards London as he announced to the German people, via a Nazi Propaganda Ministry radio correspondent, that he had 'taken over personal command of the Luftwaffe in its war against England'. His bombastic pronouncement indicates that – to him anyway – the first major attack on the British capital was more about its propaganda value than its importance as a tactical operation.

On 7 September, Göring travelled to Kesselring's advanced HQ – known as *Heiliger Berg* ('Holy Mountain'), a bombproof bunker on Cap Blanc Nez – to watch what he boasted would be the 'beginning of the end' of Dowding's Fighter Command. (NARA)

This maximum effort totalled 348 bombers accompanied by 617 Bf 109s and 31 Bf 110s. It was composed of two large formations – called 'Valhallas' by the Luftwaffe – attacking the same target five minutes apart. The first was from II. Fliegerkorps, which launched all of its 176 serviceable bombers, and was composed of three *Kampfgeschwadern* (KGs 2, 3, and 53), escorted by four *Jagdgeschwadern* (JGs 2, 3, 51, and 52). Following about half an hour later was I. Fliegerkorps' three *Kampfgeschwadern* (KGs 1, 30, and 76) flying all of their 137 serviceable bombers (augmented with 35 more from KGs 4, 26, and 54), escorted by three *Jagdgeschwadern* (JGs 26, 27, and 54). Two *Zerstörergeschwadern* (ZGs 2 and 76) would launch later to provide post-strike sweep and egress coverage for each 'Valhalla'.

Stacked from 14,000–20,000ft, the II. Fliegerkorps formation rendezvoused over the Pas de Calais and headed northwards from between Calais and Gravelines. The Swingate and Dunkirk EW radars detected the large formation at 1554hrs but it was flying perpendicular to the radars' orientation and the approaching-then-receding range information once again confused the plotters. It was not until 1616hrs, when the coastal Observer Corps stations reported 'many hundreds' of German bombers and fighters crossing the Kent coast westbound between North Foreland and Deal, that controllers at Uxbridge became aware of the raid's true position and direction. One minute later the first of 11 squadrons were 'ordered off' and, six minutes afterwards, the remaining ten were brought to five-minute 'readiness'. Conditioned by Kesseling's repeated attacks on the Sector Stations and their 'satellite airfields', six squadrons were positioned as Base CAPs overhead Biggin Hill, Croydon, and North Weald.

The tactical intent of this routing was that Loerzer's 'Valhalla' would draw Park's interceptors north and east, allowing the following I. Fliegerkorps formation a more direct route to the target area. Grauert's 'Valhalla' crossed the Channel at the narrow point – flying from Cap Gris Nez-Boulogne to cross the English coast between Dungeness and Hythe, headed north-west across Kent. Between Sevenoaks and Westerham they turned towards the centre of London. The tactic worked; once the C- and D-Sector controllers realized that the pincer attack was about to converge on London's large port facilities, they urgently

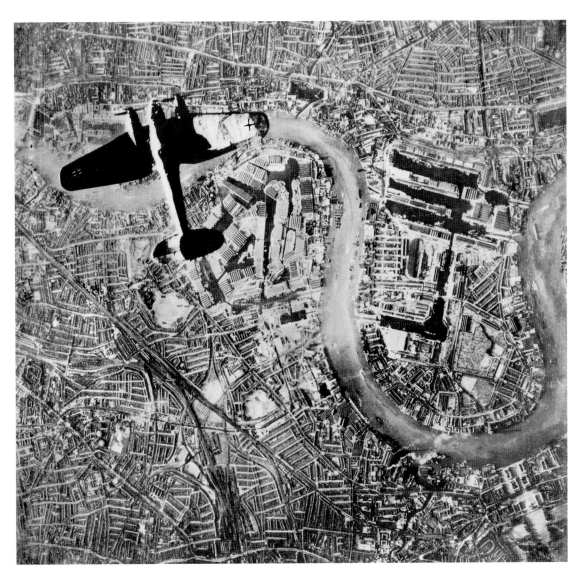

ordered the six CAP squadrons to cover Thameshaven and the Tilbury Docks. Only four units (43, 73, 249, and 303 (Polish) Sqns) were able to engage, not intercepting until the bombers reached their targets, and suffered heavy losses attempting to penetrate the massive escort screens.

From 1640–1655hrs bombs – including more than 100 of the large new SC 1800 (3,968lb) 'Satan' bombs – rained upon Woolwich Arsenal and the Surrey Docks; the oil tanks at Cliffe and Thameshaven; warehouses, granaries, and the residential areas of Rotherhithe, Limehouse, Millwall, and other districts. The large gasworks at Beckton erupted in flames and the West Ham power station was wrecked.

Leigh-Mallory's 'Duxford Wing' (19, 242, and 310 (Czech) Sqns), which had been detailed to defend F-Sector airfields, failed to rendezvous and, rushing south, engaged individually as the I. Fliegerkorps formation withdrew down the Thames Estuary. From No. 10 Group, two more units (234 and 609 Sqns) raced eastwards to attack the II. Fliegerkorps formation withdrawing across Kent, while 73 Squadron Hurricanes intercepted one of the *Zerstörer* units (ZG 2), shooting down seven Bf 110s for no loss. Other units joined in during the bombers' egress and, altogether, they shot down four Heinkels and two Ju 88s but lost

The first attack, 7 September, was a 348-bomber strike against the London's East End docks, Woolwich arsenal, and factories and oil installations along the Thames. (IWM C 5422)

Although dramatic, despite the heavy civilian casualties and the damage wrought the Luftwaffe's bombing of London was strategically insignificant and the RAF's sustained and substantial fighter opposition resulted in the disappointment, demoralization, and defeat of the Luftwaffe. (NARA)

15 Hurricanes and 13 Spitfires in doing so – a dozen pilots were killed. At least 17 of the interceptors were shot down by Bf 109s, which lost ten (plus two missing), providing a comfortable but not dramatic 1.7:1 'kill ratio'.

Göring was extremely pleased with the *Jagdwaffe's* claim of destroying 93 British interceptors – an inflation of 3.3 times the actual losses incurred. But it seems that Göring relished even more the wanton destruction of London and its suburbs, in which 448 civilians

Luftflotte 3 followed Kesselring's massive assault by sending a stream of 247 night bombers over London from 2010hrs to 0430hrs, delivering 330 tons of bombs and 440 incendiary canisters. The conflagration's huge smoke pall precluded follow-up attacks the next day. (NARA)

were killed and 1,337 injured. He gleefully reported 'London is in flames... [and] for the first time [the Luftwaffe has] delivered a stroke right into the enemy's heart.' The heavy daylight attack was followed by another 318 Luftflotte 3 bombers that, steering for the nine great conflagrations raging within London's East End, delivered 330 tons of HE and 440 incendiary canisters from 2010hrs to 0430hrs the following morning, stoking the inferno that ravaged the city for three days.

The initial attack on 15 September was by 27 Do 17Zs attempting to bomb the Battersea railway depot, followed by 52 He 111s and another 62 Do 17Zs to attack London's East End docks. (Bundesarchiv Bild 1011-341-0456-04, Photographer Folkerts)

8–14 September

The next day – since a huge pall of oily black smoke prevented striking London anyway – Luftflotte 2 returned to bombing airfields: Detling, Hornchurch, Gravesend, and West Malling were all hit in a single raid of 60 Do 17s (II. and III./KG 2). On 9 September raids against the London docks, factories at Brooklands, and RAE Farnborough were attempted, but the formations – totalling 66 bombers (KGs 1, 30 and 53) – were repulsed with the loss of ten per cent of their striking force. This defeat signalled to Hitler that air superiority was still not achieved, forcing him to postpone making a decision to initiate *Seelöwe* to 14 September, effectively 'slipping' S-Tag to 23 September.

Following a day in which weather precluded large-scale attacks, operations resumed on the 11th with Martini's *Funkhorchdienst* providing electronic jamming of four CH radars. Noise jamming is typically a contest between the power of the jammers versus the strength of the target's radar return. As formations rendezvoused over Calais, they were detectable but indiscernible – 'blotted out' – until they approached to a range at which the electronic echo 'burned through' the interference. This range proved sufficient for Park's controllers to organize their defence as some 200 bombers winged their way to attack London's docks, Brooklands' factories, Biggin Hill, Kenley, and Hornchurch. However, the nine intercepting squadrons were 'tied up' by escorting Bf 109s that pounced on them from above. Bomber loss rate was reduced by half, but it was the destruction of 28 British interceptors for the loss of seven 'Emils' that revived the Nazis' confidence that victory (defined by attaining aerial superiority) was now not so far away.

Surrey Docks

West India Docks

Royal Victoria Docks

RAF Hornchurch

LONDON

EVENTS

1. 1431hrs: having lost two Do 17Zs to colliding Hurricanes (Nos. 605 and 607 Sqns), passing abeam Chatham, Royal Navy AA fire damages five more II./KG 3 bombers.

2. 1433hrs: vectored east from overhead Hornchurch, 21 Hurricanes (Nos. 249 and 504 Squadrons) intercept II./KG 3, shooting down two Do 17Zs immediately and a third later. No losses are incurred.

3. 1435hrs: bomber formation turns towards target area, II./KG 3 takes station following KG 53.

4. 1440hrs: from CAP orbit over Chelmsford, 20 Hurricanes (Nos. 17 and 257 Sqns) intercept II./KG 26, damaging four bombers, one of them crashing near Foulness during egress. No losses are incurred.

5. 1440–1455hrs: 'Big Wing' engages. While three squadrons (Nos. 242, 302 (Polish), and 611 Sqns) engage the escorts, two others (No. 19 Sqn covered by 310 [Czech] Sqn) attack II./KG 3, shooting down one Do 17Z. Engaged by II./JG 26 and others, four Hurricanes (from 302 [Polish] and 310 (Czech] Sqns) are shot down.

6. 1444–1500hrs: vectored north from overhead Biggin Hill, 20 Spitfires (Nos. 66 and 72 Sqns) attack KG 53, followed by 21 Hurricanes (No. 1 RCAF Sqn and No. 229 Sqn) from Northolt, shooting down three bombers and damaging a fourth so badly it crash-lands at West Malling.

7. 1458–1500hrs: No. 11 Group final reserves – 23 Hurricanes (Nos. 73, 253, and 303 [Polish] Sqns) intercept II. and III./KG 2. Additionally, Nos. 17, 19, and 242 Sqns shift their attacks to KG 2. One Do 17Z is shot down and another so badly damaged it aborts mission, crashing near Chatham. One Spitfire (19 Sqn) and two Hurricanes (303 [Polish] Sqn) are lost to Bf 109E escort (I./JG 3 and I./JG 53).

8. 1445–1500hrs: 20 He 111s and 11 Do 17Zs (KG 53 and II./KG 3) arrive over Royal Victoria Docks – obscured by cloud, they drop bombs on West Ham. Five minutes later, 27 He 111s (II./KG 26) arrive over West India Docks – obscured by cloud, they bomb Bromley-by-Bow gas works. Finally, 41 Do 17Zs (KG 2) arrive over Surrey Commercial Docks – obscured by cloud, they scatter bombs across south-east London and Kent. After bomb release, all formations turn left towards Dungeness, pursued by engaged fighters and 37 fresh Spitfires and Hurricanes (Nos. 238, 602, and 609 Sqns).

KEY

 RAF Sector station

 Airfield

LUFTWAFFE UNITS

Luftflotte 2
(Note: the five groups flying 'Freie Jagd' fighter sweeps ahead of the Bomber formations have been omitted for clarity.)

1. I. and II./KG 53
2. II./KG 3
3. II./KG 26
4. III./KG 2
5. II./KG 2
6. I./JG 3
7. I./JG 53
8. I./JG 26
9. III./JG 54
10. I./JG 77
11. I./ZG 26 and V.(Z)/LG 1

Adlerangriff (Eagle Attack) phase II

The main attack, 15 September 1940

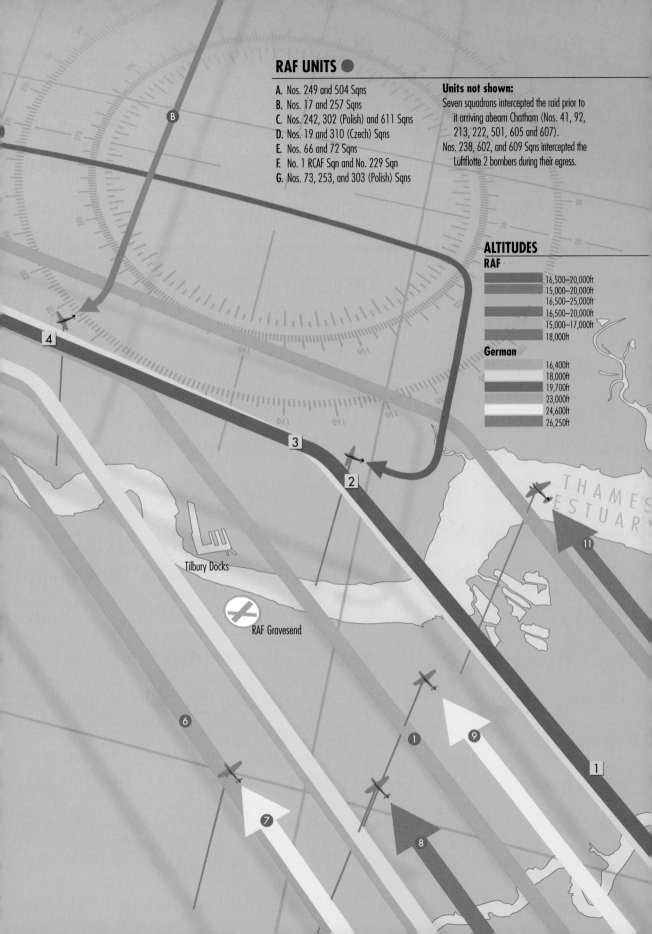

RAF UNITS ●

A. Nos. 249 and 504 Sqns
B. Nos. 17 and 257 Sqns
C. Nos. 242, 302 (Polish) and 611 Sqns
D. Nos. 19 and 310 (Czech) Sqns
E. Nos. 66 and 72 Sqns
F. No. 1 RCAF Sqn and No. 229 Sqn
G. Nos. 73, 253, and 303 (Polish) Sqns

Units not shown:
Seven squadrons intercepted the raid prior to
it arriving abeam Chatham (Nos. 41, 92,
213, 222, 501, 605 and 607).
Nos. 238, 602, and 609 Sqns intercepted the
Luftflotte 2 bombers during their egress.

ALTITUDES
RAF
16,500–20,000ft
15,000–20,000ft
16,500–25,000ft
16,500–20,000ft
15,000–17,000ft
18,000ft

German
16,400ft
18,000ft
19,700ft
23,000ft
24,600ft
26,250ft

Tilbury Docks

RAF Gravesend

THAMES
ESTUARY

On 15 September, once the three Spitfire squadrons engaged early, attempting to 'strip away' the top cover escorts, Park ordered six Hurricane squadrons to attack in pairs for maximum attrition and mutual support. These attacks shot down one Do 17Z and damaged 13 other bombers, forcing them to abort the mission. (IWM CH 1503)

Following two more days of intermittent rain and low clouds that precluded normal operations, on 14 September – blaming the weather for preventing decisively attaining the Luftwaffe's goal – Hitler postponed deciding to initiate the invasion until 17 September, delaying S-Tag to 26 September, the last possible date within the OKW 'window of opportunity' for Operation *Seelöwe*. That same afternoon, Luftflotte 2 launched limited bombing raids along with large fighter sweeps. In addition to jamming the four CH radar stations – more heavily and effectively this time – nine Ju 88s (III./KG 1) attacked three south coast radars allowing Dorniers and Heinkels to strike Brighton and Eastbourne unopposed, where 60 civilian casualties were caused. Twenty He 111s (KG 4) crossed the coast near Deal and penetrated inland over a rather expansive broken deck of cloud, intending to bomb south-east London, but the weather forced them to divert, dropping their loads on Kingston and Wimbledon, killing 49 civilians.

Park launched 22 squadrons to meet this raid but the heavy jamming handicapped the defence, the extensive cloud cover blinded the Observer Corps, and only 11 interceptors made contact with the intruders, shooting down just three Heinkels. The large *freie Jagd* accompanying this raid returned with high 'kill claims' and reported that 'the opposition appeared scrappy and uncoordinated'. At last it appeared that Dowding's Fighter Command was 'on the ropes' – one more maximum effort operation would hopefully complete its destruction.

In the week-long intermission between the two major daylight attacks on London, RAF interceptors and AA fire brought down 28 bombers while 61 Hurricanes and Spitfires were lost to Bf 109s and *Zerstörers*, which lost 22 and 11 respectively. Obviously, the revised operational strategy was working, with the 'Emil's' 'kill ratio' averaging approximately 2:1, but as with any attrition strategy, it takes time – and time was what the Luftwaffe was running out of.

15 September

Taking off from their bases near Beauvais, France, at 1010hrs, 27 Do 17Zs (I. and III./KG 76) climbed northwards and, approaching the French coast south of Boulogne, the aircrews were pleased to see approximately 100 Bf 109s (JGs 3 and 53) joining them, with about 100 more (JGs 27 and 52) sweeping out ahead. At 1050hrs the Rye CH station reported its first contact, quickly followed by several more as the fighter escorts climbed into the wide radar swath. Park brought 11 of his 21 squadrons to 'readiness', informed Brand and Leigh-Mallory, and 'ordered off' two fast-climbing Spitfire units (72 and 92 Sqns) from Biggin Hill at 1103hrs to patrol between Canterbury and Dungeness at 25,000ft.

Intending to 'stir up the defence' and weary Park's units before the main attack, *Oberstleutnant* Stefan Frölich's Dorniers crossed the English coast near Folkestone at 1135hrs as the C-Sector controller vectored the Spitfires to intercept and scrambled four squadrons, totalling 43 Hurricanes, followed by two more. Brand launched one squadron (609 Sqn) to protect Brooklands and Leigh-Mallory 'ordered off' his 'Big Wing' (19, 242, 302 (Polish), 310 (Czech), and 611 Sqns – 56 Hurricanes and Spitfires) to patrol Debden-Hornchurch.

About ten minutes later 20 Spitfires engaged the raiders over Canterbury, followed quickly by 603 Squadron, but the escorts fended them off with no losses to either side; at noon the first of three pairs of Hurricane squadrons attacked head-on as the bombers approached London. Flying over increasingly bad weather – 'seven-tenths cumulus and stratocumulus, with tops extending to 12,000ft' – the Dorniers continued towards their target: Battersea railway depot. The interceptors finally broke through the fighter screen to shoot down six Dorniers; however, the huge swirling air battle resulted in the loss of 11 Hurricanes and Spitfires. Nine 'Emils' were shot down and a tenth ditched in the Channel after combat.

Arriving in the target area at 1209hrs, Frölich's bomb-aimers found a sizeable hole in the dense cloud and dropped most of their 23 tons of bombs through it, cutting the tracks at the Pouparts Viaduct and halting all rail traffic, and killing 24 people. As the Dorniers crossed the capital and wheeled south-east, Sqn Ldr Douglas Bader led the 'Big Wing' in a flank attack that resulted in a running battle, chasing the ragged formation towards the Kent coastline, but without notable success.

While Frölich's raid opened the day's battle, Kesselring's much larger follow-up attack planned to do major damage to three large commercial dockyards in London's East End in

Meeting the 'Big Wing'

'Here they come... the last fifty Spitfires...'
Anonymous Kampfflieger crewmember, upon seeing the approach of the 'Big Wing', 15 September, 1940

In retrospect, Luftflotte 2's air attack on London's East End dockyards on 15 September 1940 is generally viewed as the climax of the 'Battle of Britain', and in some ways it was. With the Luftwaffe's bomber strength waning, it was desperately hoped that RAF Fighter Command was in a similar situation and – according to the assurances of ObdL Intelligence – it was a 'spent force'. However, the strike force's encounter with No. 12 Group's 'Big Wing' over London that day came as a profound and devastating shock to the morale and hopes of the Luftwaffe.

As the 114 bombers crossed the English coastline, AVM Park's C-Sector controller employed Dowding's doctrine of 'intercept early and attrite heavily' with nine squadrons attacking in sequences over a 20–25 minute period, shooting down or turning back 14 bombers – 12.28 per cent of the strike force. AVM Leigh-Mallory's highly-touted 'Big Wing' was held back in case the strike force was feinting towards London but intended to bomb North Weald, Debden and other targets north-east of the capital. The five-squadron 'Big Wing' was amongst the 13 units intercepting the strike force in the target area, shooting down 11 bombers, four of them known to have fallen to the 'Big Wing's' Spitfires and Hurricanes.

Seen here approaching the target area, one of the leading bombers – He 111H-3 A1+DA from Stab/KG 53 – is being attacked head-on by No. 242 Squadron Hurricanes. These were led by the indomitable Sqn Ldr Douglas Bader, flying Hurricane I LE●D/V7467, seen attacking bombers out of view to the right. The Heinkel, crewed by *Feldwebels* Benz, Cionber, and Schweiger and *Uffz* Meier and Geiger, was hit by subsequent attacks and, within two minutes, caught fire and crashed near Tripcot Pier, Woolwich Arsenal, just west of the target area, killing all aboard.

GRAHAM TURNER '16

After running a gauntlet of nine squadrons from the coast to the target area, the main raid on 15 September was engaged head-on by 13 squadrons of Hurricanes and Spitfires over London's East End, including No. 12 Group's 'Big Wing', finally shattering the illusion that Fighter Command was a defeated foe. (IWM CH 740)

an effort to lure Fighter Command into a decisive engagement. The strike force was led by *Oberst* Erich Stahl's KG 53, with the Do 17s of Fink's II. and III./KG 2 in column on the left and Fuchs' newly arrived II./KG 26 following II./KG 3 on the right. As they assembled, JG 26 and JG 51 ranged ahead on a large *freie Jagd* sweep while six *Jagdgruppen* (I.[J]/LG 2 and five from JGs 3, 26, 53, and 77) climbed above the bomber formations to fly 'top cover'. III./JG 54 flew close escort while 20 *Zerstörers* (I./ZG 26 and V.(Z)/LG 1) took station on the right. Covered by 360 fighters, the 114 medium and light bombers headed towards London's East End docks in a 6.5-mile-wide formation, crossing the Channel westbound, pointing at Dungeness before turning north-west towards their targets.

They were detected at 1345hrs and 15 minutes later Park began launching his interceptors again, eventually scrambling sections and flights of all 21 squadrons – 185 Spitfires and Hurricanes – to meet Stahl's aerial armada. At 1415hrs, the C-Sector controller opened his attacks with three Spitfire units (41, 92, and 222 Sqns), then – at five-minute intervals – three pairs of Hurricane squadrons (213/607, 501/605, and 249/504 Sqns) engaged. These were effectively countered by the escorts, allowing 100 bombers to reach the target area with their formations intact before Park's main force (eight squadrons) and reserves (three squadrons) arrived, reinforced by Leigh-Mallory's 'Big Wing' (now 47 interceptors). However, the raiders were unable to locate the individual dockyards due to weather and dropped most of their bombs on West Ham, Bromley-by-Bow, and adjacent areas before turning towards home.

Because many of the escorts had been 'stripped away' as they fought their way across Kent, the bombers were particularly vulnerable in the target area and during egress, with a total of 14 Do 17Zs and seven He 111Hs being shot down, while the defenders lost nine Hurricanes and three Spitfires, half of them to Bf 109s. Luftflotte 2 lost 12 'Emils' to defending fighters and three *Zerstörers* were also shot down.

About the same time, Sperrle's Luftflotte 3 mounted its two, much smaller, raids. From Villacoublay, 27 He 111Ps (III./KG 55) steered initially towards Southampton, but as they

approached, they turned west to attack Portland naval base. With *Seelöwe* scheduled to begin two days hence, this raid was designed to deter the RN's return to threaten the cross-Channel operation. Little damage was done – only five bombs fell within the naval installations – and the raid was intercepted by six Spitfires (152 Sqn), which shot down one Heinkel. This was followed almost two hours later by 18 Bf 110 *Jabos* (1. and 2./ErprGr 210) making a surprise low-level attack on Vickers-Supermarine's Spitfire factory at Woolston – no hits were scored and no losses suffered.

Overall, the two Luftflotten flew 218 bomber and 799 fighter sorties, losing 32 bombers (including a weather reconnaissance aircraft) and 26 fighters – a total of 58 aircraft. The Luftwaffe's leadership expected much of this day's attacks – ObdL had predicted it to be 'the decisive blow'. It was decisive, although not in the way Göring and his staff anticipated. The fighter exchange rate – the basis upon which Göring's hopes were pinned – was even, a 1:1 ratio, and bomber losses were nearly 15 per cent, a completely prohibitive and unsustainable rate of attrition.

Although the battles of 15 September dealt a severe blow to the confidence of Göring and the Luftwaffe, British wartime propaganda – and the histories that followed – vastly overrated the magnitude of the RAF's success. Fighter Command issued a statement to the BBC – which broadcast it nationwide, forever cementing this misinformation into the canon of Battle of Britain mythology – saying that its interceptor pilots and AA gunners had shot down 185 German raiders. (After the war, the 'error' was corrected by reducing the claim to 60 German aircraft destroyed, a number very close to accurate, but by this time the British public had little interest in correcting the record.) It was, however, a much-needed tonic for the flagging morale of the RAF and the increasing frustration, dissatisfaction, and worry of the British public. Coupled with the subsequent cancellation[6] of Operation *Seelöwe*, which reinforced the perception of high drama, the propaganda ploy proved eminently successful, and resulted in the annual celebration of 15 September as 'Battle of Britain Day'.

But to the chronically fatigued RAF pilots and acutely frustrated Luftwaffe aircrew alike, it was only another bitter day in an exhausting series of daily battles. The campaign continued, but took yet another turn.

With the defeat of the Luftwaffe's bomber forces in massed attacks at medium level, and encouraged by ErprGr 210's success, ObdL attempted to substitute Bf 109E-4s and E-7s making small harassment raids on London. Each *Jagdgeschwader* was ordered to form three squadrons (one in each *gruppe*) of *Jabos*. During October 2,633 *Jabo* sorties were flown in 140 individual attacks. (Private Collection)

6 Technically an 'indefinite postponement', but the result was the same.

The end of *Adlerangriff*

'Robinson', Göring's ObdL mobile HQ, steamed into Boulogne railway station on 15 September and the next day the *Reichsmarschall* hosted his last '*Adlerangriff Besprechung*'. Dismayed by the results of the previous day's operation, he predicted 'with four or five days of heavy losses he [the RAF] ought to be finished off…' *Generalmajor* Theodor Osterkamp, the new Jagdfliegerführer 2 commander, shared his *Jagdwaffe* pilots' report of encountering Bader's 'Big Wing': 'The English have adopted new tactics. They are now using powerful fighter formations to attack in force… Yesterday these new tactics took us by surprise.' Unwilling to entertain dissent in urging his commanders to press their attacks on London, Göring's response was 'That's just what we want! If they come at us in droves, we can shoot them down in droves.'

But Göring did not have 'four or five days' to complete the destruction of Fighter Command. On 17 September, Hitler postponed *Seelöwe* indefinitely. With no invasion to support, *Adlerangriff* – as an OCA campaign – was over. Defeated, but not yet willing to admit it, Göring pressed his commanders to continue their bombing of London (by Luftflotte 2) and British aviation industry targets (Luftflotte 3). His vain, desperate hope was 'to bring England to terms by the Luftwaffe's independent impact on morale and economy.' While not harbouring such sanguine expectations, Hitler did not want to relieve the pressure on the British government or its populace for fear that *Seelöwe*'s cancellation might be discerned.

Göring got his 'four or five days' of heavy attacks during the final week of September. On the 25th, Kesselring launched 275 bomber sorties to attack London while Sperrle sent 58 He 111s (KG 55) to bomb the Bristol factory at Filton, destroying eight new Blenheims and Beaufighters and damaging a dozen more, causing 357 casualties and halting production for several weeks. The following day 59 Heinkels (KG 55 again), with a strong fighter escort, dropped 70 tons of bombs on the Supermarine factory at Woolston, causing 89 casualties, destroying three Spitfires and damaging 20 more, and also stopping production temporarily.

Next day Kesselring launched three waves against London while Sperrle again struck Bristol, but most raiders were repulsed with heavy losses before reaching their targets. Finally, on 30 September, Kesselring sent 173 bombers – escorted by 1,000 fighter sorties – in two waves against London while Sperrle despatched 40 Heinkels (KG 55) to bomb the Westland factory at Yeovil. Only 30 bombers (KG 30) made it through to London, where damage was light, and Luftflotte 3's attack was spoilt by cloud. Intercepting Hurricanes and Spitfires significantly outperformed their opponents, shooting down 16 bombers and 27 Bf 109s for the loss of only 16 of their own. According to Adolf Galland, 'Göring was shattered. He simply could not understand how the increasingly painful loss of bombers came about.'

Following this, the last great daylight battle over London, massed formations virtually disappeared and daytime raids steadily decreased. Beginning on 7 September, Göring had altered the operational strategy to a battle of attrition. It was a battle that the Luftwaffe could not win. Exactly one month later, the two Luftflotten were reduced to about 800 bombers (down from 1,131) and approximately 600 fighters (down from 813). To make matters worse, serviceability was seriously affected. Due to the lack of an effective field maintenance/repair capability, seriously damaged aircraft had to be returned by rail or truck to the unit's home base in Germany, or they were cannibalized to keep other aircraft operational. Consequently, of the above figures only 52 per cent of the bombers and 68 per cent of the fighters remained operational. It proved to be a defeat from which the Luftwaffe would never recover.

AFTERMATH AND ANALYSIS

The enemy air force is still by no means defeated; on the contrary, it shows increasing activity. The weather situation as a whole does not permit us to expect a period of calm. The Führer, therefore, decided to postpone *Unternehmen Seelöwe* indefinitely.

Kriegsmarine *Seekriegsleitung* (Navy War Staff) War Diary, September 17, 1940

Following the Luftwaffe's final defeat on the last day of September, daytime fighting – apart from the increasing but operationally ineffective *Jabo* 'tip-and-run' raids – continued in desultory fashion until 29 October, when a dozen Junkers Ju 88As (I./LG 1) raided Portland. It was the last daylight attack on Britain by Luftwaffe bombers. Consequently, and officially for the RAF, the Battle of Britain ended on 31 October 1940.

Meanwhile, the night bombing campaign – which was coincidental but never really part of *Adlerangriff* proper – continued through the winter and the following springtime. Attempting to comply with Hitler's Directives Nr. 9 and 13, the Luftwaffe's night bombing of Britain began on 2/3 June, with small formations targeting British industrial areas, shifting later that month to aircraft factory and airfield locations. Using the 42–48MHz *Knickebein* ('crooked leg') radio-beam long-range navigation system, Luftwaffe night bombing proved far more accurate than the concurrent RAF nocturnal operations. Over the next ten weeks 16 industrial plants, 14 ports and 13 airfields were targeted.

When Göring decided to focus daylight attacks against No. 11 Group's airfields, Sperrle's Luftflotte 3 transitioned almost exclusively to nocturnal operations. In the last week of August Sperrle doubled heavy attacks on southern and western ports, especially Merseyside, delivering 496 tons of bombs in 629 sorties during a sustained four-night bombardment.

Fighter Command's night intercept capability was in its infancy and its radar system was generally ineffective over land, so Luftwaffe losses were few. Göring's 3 September orders

The main reason that the Luftwaffe lost the battle of attrition during the latter phases of *Adlerangriff* was because, despite their high losses and unfavourable 'exchange rate' against the Bf 109E, British fighter production exceeded the German production of the 'Emil' three-fold. (NARA)

Despite being defeated, the Luftwaffe continued the Battle of Britain with the 'Night Blitz' in which London was bombed on 57 consecutive nights in a 'punishment campaign' (*Strafe Angriff*) that killed 40,000 civilians. (NARA)

made London the primary target and Sperrle's first attack was by 70 bombers on the night of 5/6 September. Beginning two nights later, London was bombed on 57 consecutive nights, destroying and damaging more than one million homes and killing more than 40,000 civilians.

Even after the disheartening battles of 15 and 30 September, Sperrle's night raids continued – more as punishment (*Strafe Angriff*) than for any strategic or operational purpose. During the next 34 weeks London was bombed 48 times, with multiple major attacks also hitting Birmingham, Liverpool, Plymouth, Bristol, Glasgow, Southampton, Portsmouth and Hull, while eight other cities were bombed once – killing another 20,000 British citizens. This 'Night Blitz' lasted until 21 May 1941 when the Luftwaffe had to reorganize and deploy eastwards for *Unternehmen Barbarossa* ('Operation *Barbarossa*'), the Nazi invasion of Soviet Russia, slated to commence one month later.

Initially the night bombardment was intended to 'blockade' Britain by destructively closing its port facilities while U-boats interdicted inbound shipping at sea. As previously noted, Luftwaffe doctrine and leadership originally considered this the only means of 'strategic air attack' to hold any promise for a decisive outcome. However, like siege warfare, a 'blockade strategy' – or even an all-out 'strategic attack' – takes months of persistent effort to be effective. Instead, Hitler was unwilling to engage in a long war against Britain, despite the facts that this was precisely the basis of pre-war planning, the stated rationale for the invasion of France and the Low Countries, and the Luftwaffe's preferred manner of conducting strategic aerial warfare. Hitler's lack of patience resulted in his determination that 'A successful landing followed by occupation would end the war in short order… A long war is undesirable for us.' The Luftwaffe was to facilitate the cross-Channel operation by attaining aerial superiority over the southern coast of England. But this was a hasty expedient and a poor substitute for a sound long-term strategy.

The failings of the Luftwaffe in attempting this OCA campaign have been discussed by others and mentioned previously in this account: the lack of a command-level planning staff;

shallow, simple, superficial, and misleading intelligence summaries; and inadequate photo-reconnaissance. These deficiencies forced the Luftflotten staffs to do their own – largely independent – operational planning, intelligence assessments, and reconnaissance, resulting in essentially two separate campaigns. The best example of this is the opening attacks against CH radar stations. Luftflotte 3 hit Ventnor with 15 bombs from dive-bombing Ju 88s – knocking it out for three days – while Luftflotte 2 hit four radar sites with three or four bombs delivered by *Jabos*, shutting them down for just three to six hours.

Unlike other military campaigns, the success of an air campaign cannot be assessed by cities captured, territory occupied, or enemy armies defeated or destroyed. Instead, an air campaign's success or failure hinges upon whether it attained its assigned objectives or stated aims. Moreover, an air campaign cannot be graded by comparing opposing sides' aerial victory claims or aggregate losses.

'Kill claims' are only an indication of the intensity of aerial combat, not the actual numbers of opposing aircraft destroyed. They fuel wartime propaganda and are frequently sensationalized by amateur historians and aviation enthusiasts, but they are valueless to professional military historians because they are always – and usually grossly – inflated. In this campaign, Luftwaffe 'victory claims' were 2.57 to 3.32 times more than RAF losses. Fighter Command claims were similarly inflated. On two of the heaviest days of fighting (15 and 18 August), the RAF claimed 336 Luftwaffe aircraft shot down when actually 143 were lost – an over-claim rate of 238 per cent. On 'Battle of Britain Day' Fighter Command over-claimed by 325 per cent.

Likewise, for the military historian, daily aggregate losses – including all losses of all types to all causes – are almost as meaningless. The only numbers that matter are the actual losses in combat – as used in this account – and the rate of replacement of those losses. In the case of the Battle of Britain, the Luftwaffe 'won' the former (the 'Emil's' overall exchange ratio from 12 August through 15 September was 1.77:1), destroying slightly more than three RAF fighters for every two Bf 109Es lost. However, with British factories producing three times as many replacements as Messerschmitt (along with Erla, Arado and Fieseler) each month, the *Jagdwaffe's* marginal superiority was insufficient to destroy Fighter Command. The resulting maths reveal that, as a 'fighter-versus-fighter battle' or 'battle of attrition', for the Luftwaffe the 'Battle of Britain' was never a winnable contest.

Because of the *Jagdwaffe's* chronic over-claiming and ObdL's lame intelligence assessments, Luftwaffe leadership was blinded to the fact that it was losing this 'battle of attrition' until the dramatic encounter with Leigh-Mallory's 'Big Wing' on 15 September. Although inconsistent with Dowding's doctrine and Park's practice of 'intercept early and attrite heavily', the psychological impact of five squadrons of Hurricanes and Spitfires clashing head-on with Kesselring's last large bomber attack on London shook Göring and the Luftwaffe's leadership to their very core. Having lost 508 bombers and 668 fighters (Bf 109s and 110s), it was shocking and crushingly disheartening to realize that RAF Fighter Command remained a strong and viable opponent.

Göring's elemental error of attempting to engage Fighter Command in the 'battle of attrition' over London frequently masks the fundamental fact that the main flaw in *Adlerangriff's* execution was the Luftwaffe's lack of persistence in its attacks. The best examples of this are the sporadic and frequently lightweight attacks against the CH radar network and the premature abandonment of attacks against Park's Sector Stations.

In seven days that included 11 attacks, Biggin Hill was reduced to operating only a 'local defence flight' while many of the station's sections and the all-important Sector Operations Room were relocated off the aerodrome. Although minimum capability was re-established within 12 hours, C-Sector's squadrons were reassigned to neighbouring sectors for a week while communications and operations capabilities were restored to near normal levels. If, after effectively neutralizing Biggin Hill, Kesselring had been allowed to shift his attacks

Then one day, they came no more. (NARA)

to the adjacent B-Sector (this had already begun), after a similar effort it is reasonable to expect that Kenley would have been similarly disabled by 12 September, just in time for *Seelöwe* to begin. Neutralizing Hornchurch would have followed.

It is instructive to modern air defence networks that Britain's IADS – as primitive as it was in 1940 – proved resilient and could absorb the neutralization of one Sector Station and still function effectively. But the loss of two adjacent Sector Stations would probably have proven debilitating to the co-ordinated air defence of the south-east quadrant of No. 11 Group's AOR. This is precisely what Park became anxious about. He wrote on 12 September, 'There was a critical period between 28 August and 5 September when the damage to Sector Stations and our ground organization was having a serious effect on the fighting efficiency of the fighter squadrons.' At this point Dowding came to the conclusion that, should the pounding continue, he 'had no alternative but to withdraw 11 Group from south-east England altogether'. Due to the restricted range of the Spitfire, launching from airfields north of the Thames would have moved the aerial battlefield to over northern Kent, thus conceding aerial superiority over the Channel as well as the ports and beaches of southern Kent and Sussex, and thereby giving the victory to Göring.

Park's and Dowding's concerns indicate that, with diligence and persistence, the 'Battle of Britain' could have indeed been won by the Luftwaffe, and would have gone into the books as history's first successful independent air campaign. However, spurred by the increasing angst associated with the looming deadline for launching Operation *Seelöwe*, an egocentric and power-hungry politician with the veneer credibility of a military aviator's war record, but with no concept of modern combat or air campaigning, made a fateful decision that cost the Luftwaffe its potential for victory. In giving the victory to Dowding and Fighter Command, Göring assured the survival of Great Britain and, with it, gave Western civilization the chance to eventually destroy Nazi Germany.

BIBLIOGRAPHY AND FURTHER READING

It is commonly supposed that a heavily outnumbered Royal Air Force, by sheer gallantry and skill, achieved a well-nigh miraculous victory.

Telford Taylor, *The Breaking Wave: The German Defeat in the Summer of 1940*

Except for Waterloo, the Battle of Britain is very likely the most written about conflict in English historical literature. In the 75 years following this unprecedented clash of air forces, it has been recounted by historians including Edward Bishop (1960), Wood and Dempster (1961), Basil Collier (1962), Richard Collier (1966), Francis K. Mason (1969), and even novelist Len Deighton (1977). Unfortunately, most of the earliest accounts use as part of their basis the Air Ministry's 1941 92-page booklet (officially Pamphlet 156) on the 'Battle of Britain' (reprinted in 1989 in anticipation of the 50th Anniversary of the Battle); consequently in many cases wartime propaganda has been confused with, and for, historical fact.

Subsequent histories – frequently only parroting the earlier accounts in different prose – almost universally failed to consult detailed German records, other than command-level documentation and individual participants' personal experiences, creating voids filled with supposition and mistaken RAF-sourced information. Simultaneously, the frequent retelling of the resulting legend has caused a 'transfiguration' of sorts, elevating Dowding as saviour, Park to the papal seat, and canonizing 'The Few'. To discuss this tenaciously fought aerial clash in any other terms is commonly considered sacrilege.

The greatest fault of all of these is their lack of use of documented German sources. The notable exception to this trend are the works of Dr Alfred Price, whose more narrowly focussed accounts are the epitome of thoroughly researched and objectively presented history. With diligent life-long research by a wide variety of lesser known modern-day aviation historians – Peter Cornell, Donald Caldwell, Chris Goss, John Vasco, Richard Smith and Eddie Creek, and Henry de Zeng and Douglas Stankey – a large number of very useful and revealing sources of individual unit and aircraft-type histories have resulted.

Other than Price and Osprey's prolific John Weal, most mainstream authors have neglected the Bundesarchiv-Militärachiv's documents held at Freiburg, at least until Stephen Bungay wrote *The Most Dangerous Enemy* (Aurum Press, 2001). While Bungay's account is the best yet – the 2010 reprinting tagline bragged that it was 'The Definitive History of the Battle of Britain' – and is written in crisp, modern, very readable prose, it suffers from technical and historical errors in the chapters leading up to *Adlertag*. Thereafter, it is excellent when including German source information, but it still regurgitates the proliferate errors contained in the Battle's Arthurian-like lore when they are not corrected by the opposing side's data.

Naturally there are few English-language histories providing the Germans' view of the campaign – it was a defeat after all. The sole known published German-language account is Dr Theo Weber's *Die Luftschlact um England* (Huber, 1956). The earliest and best examination of *Adlerangriff* and *Seelöwe* at all command levels was by American historian Telford Taylor in *The Breaking Wave: the German defeat in the summer of 1940* (Weidenfeld & Nicolson, 1967). British historian E. R. Hooten's *Eagle in Flames: The Fall of the Luftwaffe* (W & N, 1997) contains an excellent section on the Luftwaffe's decision-making and operations during the campaign. German historian Hans-Dieter Berenbrok (aka 'Cajus Bekker') includes a substantial, but selective and largely 'oral', section in his famous *The Luftwaffe War Diaries: The German Air Force in World War II* (Ballantine Books, 1966). The best is Karl Klee's chapter 'The Battle of Britain' in Jacobsen and Rohwer's translated compendium *Decisive Battles of World War II* (Putnam, 1965). Klee was also the author of one of the USAF's Historical Studies, #157 'Operation "Sea Lion" and the Role Planned for the Luftwaffe' (USAF Historical Division: 1955) which, along with Andreas Nielsen's Study #173 'German Air Force General Staff' (1959), resides at Maxwell AFB, Alabama, among informative studies prepared by such notable Luftwaffe officers as Paul Deichmann, Wilhelm Speidel, Richard Suchenwirth, and Joseph Kammhuber. These, along with the 'Von Rohden Collection' at the US National Archive and Records Administration, are sources commonly neglected by most Battle of Britain historians.

The following proved useful in compiling this account:

Berenbrok, Hans-Dieter (writing as Cajus Bekker) *The Luftwaffe War Diaries: The German Air Force in World War II*, Doubleday & Company, New York (1968)

Bungay, Stephen, *The Most Dangerous Enemy: A History of the Battle of Britain*, Aurum Press Ltd ,London (2015)

Cooper, Matthew, *The German Air Force 1033–1945: An Anatomy of Failure*, Jane's Publishing Incorporated, New York (1981)

Cornwell, Peter D., *The Battle of Britain Then and Now*, Battle of Britain International Ltd, Old Harlow, UK (2006)

Corum, James S., *The Luftwaffe: Creating the Operational Air War, 1918–1940*, University Press of Kansas, Lawrence, KS (1997)

Goss, Chris, *Luftwaffe Fighter-Bombers over Britain: The Tip-and-Run Campaign, 1942–43*, Stackpole Books, Mechanicsburg, VA (2010)

Hooten, E. R., *Eagle in Flames: The Fall of the Luftwaffe*, Brockhampton Press, London, (1999)

Klee, Karl, 'Operation "Sea Lion" and the Role Planned for the Luftwaffe,' unpublished USAF Study No. 157, Monograph 8-1115-6, USAF Historical Division, Maxwell AFB, AL, (1955)

Mason, Francis K., *Battle over Britain*, Aston Publications Ltd, Bourne End, UK (1990)

Mombeek, Eric, with J. Richard Smith and Eddie J. Creek, *Luftwaffe Colours: Jagdwaffe Volume Two – Battle of Britain*, Classic Publications Limited, Crowborough, UK (2001)

Price, Alfred, Dr, *Battle of Britain Day: 15 September 1940*, Sidgwick & Jackson, London (1990)

Price, Alfred, *Battle of Britain: The Hardest Day, 18 August 1940*, Charles Scribner's Sons, New York (1979)

Price, Alfred, Dr, *The Luftwaffe Data Book*, Stackpole Books, Mechanicsburg, PA (1997)

Smith, J. Richard, and Eddie J. Creek, *Kampfflieger Volume One: Bombers of the Luftwaffe 1933–1940* and *Volume Two: Bombers of the Luftwaffe July 1940-December 1941*, Ian Allan Printing Ltd, Hersham, UK (2004)

Taylor, Telford, *The Breaking Wave: The German defeat in the summer of 1940*, Weidenfeld & Nicolson, London (1967)

Vasco, John J., and Peter D. Cornwell, *Zerstörer: The Messerschmitt 110 and its Units in 1940*, JAC Publications, Drayton, UK (1995)

Wood, Derek and Derek Dempster, *The Narrow Margin*, Third Edition, Smithsonian Institute Press, Washington, D.C. (1990)

Zeng IV, Henry L. de, and Douglas G. Stankey, *Bomber Units of the Luftwaffe 1933–1945: A Reference Source, Volumes 1* and *2* and *Dive-Bomber and Ground-Attack Units of the Luftwaffe 1933–1945: A Reference Source, Volumes 1* and *2,* Midland Publishing, Hinkley, UK (2007 through 2010)

INDEX